A SECOND SUPPLEMENTARY HAND-LIST OF THE MUḤAMMADAN MANUSCRIPTS IN THE UNIVERSITY AND COLLEGES OF CAMBRIDGE

A SECOND SUPPLEMENTARY HAND-LIST OF THE MUHAMMADAN MANUSCRIPTS IN THE UNIVERSITY & COLLEGES OF CAMBRIDGE

BY

A. J. ARBERRY

LITT.D., F.B.A.,

Sir Thomas Adams's Professor of Arabic
Fellow of Pembroke College, Cambridge

CAMBRIDGE
AT THE UNIVERSITY PRESS
1952

CAMBRIDGE UNIVERSITY PRESS
Cambridge, New York, Melbourne, Madrid, Cape Town,
Singapore, São Paulo, Delhi, Mexico City

Cambridge University Press
The Edinburgh Building, Cambridge CB2 8RU, UK

Published in the United States of America by Cambridge University Press, New York

www.cambridge.org
Information on this title: www.cambridge.org/9781107623859

First published 1952
First paperback edition 2013

A catalogue record for this publication is available from the British Library

ISBN 978-1-107-62385-9 Paperback

PREFACE

The name of Edward Granville Browne will always live in the annals of Cambridge University Library not only because he wrote the catalogues of the Mohammedan manuscripts (of which this small volume is a continuation), and not only because he gave his own splendid collection to the Library. In addition to these most notable contributions and benefactions, he also bequeathed a sum of money for the purchase of books and manuscripts relating to Islam; and a substantial proportion of the volumes listed in these pages came into the Library's possession as a result of that bequest.

E. G. Browne's successor in the Sir Thomas Adams's Chair of Arabic, Reynold Alleyne Nicholson, being ambitious to continue the tradition of his revered teacher and beloved friend, in his own turn willed to the Library the valuable manuscripts which he had inherited from his grandfather John Nicholson, to which he added other volumes he himself acquired. The R. A. Nicholson bequest is the most important of its kind that the Library has received since E. G. Browne's gift came in. During these twenty-five years other benefactors have also enriched the Islamic collection, and their names are recorded in due place.

This handlist has been compiled upon economic lines; but though austere, it will be found to contain the references adequate to establish the identity and significance of each item. The compiler desires to record his obligation and thanks to Mr Naish, formerly in charge of the oriental department of the Library, who made the index and helped in many other ways.

A. J. A.

1 (a) **Or. 951 (10)**

Notes on the *Dīwān* of Bahā' al-Dīn Abu 'l-Faḍl Zuhair b. Muḥammad al-Muhallabī (d. 656/1258), by E. H. Palmer (d. 1882).

Ff. 209. Clear naskh. 19th century. Presented by E. G. Browne.

2 (p, u) **Or. 986 (11)**

1. *Rāziq Bārī*, by Ismā'īl, a Persian-Urdu rhymed vocabulary. Ff. 1–12.
2. A treatise on arithmetic. Ff. 13–33.
3. A tract on the Mahratta army. Ff. 34–41.
4. A Fragment. Ff. 42–45.

Ff. 45. Clear nasta'līq. 12/18th century.

3 (a) **Or. 995 (9)**

1. *Intikhāb al-Iqtiḍāb*, by Abū Naṣr Sa'īd b. Abi'l-Khair al-Masīḥī b. 'Īsā al-Mutaṭabbib (d. 589/1193). Ff. 1–51a. Brockelmann, Suppl. I, 893.
2. *Al-Rauḍat al-tibbīya*, by Abū Sa'īd 'Ubaid Allāh b. Jibrīl Ibn Bukhtīshū' (d. *ca.* 450/1058). Ff. 51*b*–73. Printed at Cairo, 1927. Brockelmann I, 236, 483; Suppl. I, 886.

Ff. 73. Excellent naskh. 9/15th century.

4 (a) **Or. 996 (8)**

Al-Intikhāb li-kashf al-abyāt al-mushkilat al-i'rāb, by 'Afīf al-Dīn Abu'l-Ḥasan 'Alī b. 'Adlān b. Ḥammād b. 'Alī al-Mauṣilī (d. 666/1268).

Ff. 32. Excellent scholar's naskh. 16 Rajab 720/23 Aug. 1320. No other copy appears to be recorded.

5 (a) **Or. 997 (13)**

Anwār al-rabī' fī anwā' al-badī', by Ṣadr al-Dīn 'Alī-Khān b. Aḥmad Ibn Muḥammad Ma'ṣūm al-Ḥusainī al-Ḥasanī al-Madanī (d. 1117/1705 or 1120/1708).

Ff. 248. Scholar's naskh. 12/18th century. Printed at Teheran, 1314/1896. Brockelmann II, 421; Suppl. II, 628.

6 (a) **Or. 998** (8)

Al-Īḍāḥ fī 'ilm al-balāgha, by Jalāl al-Dīn Abu 'l-Ma'ālī Muḥammad b. 'Abd al-Raḥmān Khaṭīb Dimashq al-Qazwīnī (d. 739/1338).

Ff. 141. Scholar's naskh. Rajab 742/Dec.–Jan. 1341–2. Printed at Fez. Brockelmann I, 294; Suppl. I, 516.

7 (a) **Or. 999** (12)

Al-Baḥr al-zakhkhār al-jāmi' li-madhāhib 'ulamā' al-amṣār, by Aḥmad b. Yaḥyā Ibn al-Murtaḍā al-Mahdī li-dīn Allāh (d. 840/1437).

Ff. 317. Excellent Yemeni naskh. Rabī' I, 1046/Aug. 1636. Brockelmann II, 187; Suppl. II, 245.

8 (a) **Or. 1000** (8)

Al-Baḥr al-maurūd fi 'l-mawāthīq wa'l-'uhūd, by Abu 'l-Mawāhib 'Abd al-Wahhāb b. Aḥmad b. 'Alī al-Sha'rānī al-Shāfi'ī (d. 973/1565).

Ff. 144. Clear naskh. 19 Sha'bān 1054/22 Oct. 1644. Printed at Cairo, 1278/1862, 1287/1870, 1321/1903. Brockelmann II, 337; Suppl. II, 465.

9 (a) **Or. 1001** (9)

Al-Burhān fī 'alāmāt al-Mahdī ākhir al-zamān, by 'Alā' al-Dīn 'Alī b. Ḥusām al-Dīn 'Abd al-Malik b. Qāḍī-Khān al-Muttaqī al-Hindī al-Jaunpūrī (d. 975/1567 or 977/1569).

Ff. 53. Scholar's naskh. 27 Ramaḍān 1175/22 April 1762. Brockelmann II, 384; Suppl. II, 518.

10 (a) **Or. 1002** (12)

Jawāmi' al-jāmi' fī tafsīr al-Qur'ān, by Raḍī al-Dīn Abū 'Alī al-Faḍl b. al-Ḥasan al-Ṭabarsī (d. 548/1153 or 552/1158).

Ff. 408. Excellent naskh. 28 Rabī' II 1121/7 July 1709. Printed at Teheran, 1321/1903, Qumm, 1902. Brockelmann I, 405; Suppl. I, 709.

11 (a) **Or. 1003** (9)

Thamarāt al-aurāq, by Taqī al-Dīn Abu'l-Maḥāsin Abū Bakr b. 'Alī b. 'Abd Allāh Ibn Ḥijja al-Ḥamawī al-Qādirī al-Ḥanafī (d. 837/1434).

Ff. 208. Fine scholar's naskh. 9/15th century. Illuminated title-page and 'unwān. Printed at Cairo, 1300/1882, 1308/1890, 1320–1/1902–1903. Brockelmann II, 16; Suppl. II, 9.

12 (a) **Or. 1004 (8)**

Al-Jāmi' al-akbar wa'l-baḥr al-azkhar (part 13), by Muwaffaq al-Dīn Abu'l-Qāsim 'Īsā b. 'Abd al-'Azīz b. 'Īsā al-Iskandarānī al-Lakhmī (d. 629/1231).

Ff. 90. Old cursive naskh. 614/1217–18. No other copy appears to be preserved, *see* Brockelmann I, 303; Suppl. I, 531.

13 (a) **Or. 1005 (9)**

Al-Jāmi' al-ṣaghīr, by Ḥusām al-Dīn 'Umar b. 'Abd al-'Azīz b. Māza al-Ṣadr al-Shahīd al-Bukhārī (d. 536/1141).

Ff. 219. Scholar's naskh. 724/1323–4. Brockelmann I, 374; Suppl. I, 640.

14 (a) **Or. 1006 (9)**

Ḥilyat al-abrār wa-shi'ār al-akhyār, by Muḥyī al-Dīn Abū Zakarīyā' Yaḥyā b. Sharaf b. Mūrī al-Nawawī (d. 676/1278).

Ff. 147. Scholar's ta'līq. Rabī' I 993/March 1585. Printed at Cairo, 1300/1882, 1312/1894, 1331/1912. Brockelmann, Suppl. I, 685.

15 (a) **Or. 1007 (11)**

Al-Risāla ila'l-Ṣūfīya, by Abu'l-Qāsim 'Abd al-Karīm b. Hawāzin b. 'Abd al-Malik al-Qushairī (d. 465/1072).

Ff. 231. Fine old scholar's naskh. 2 Ramaḍān 731/9 June 1331. Printed frequently. Brockelmann I, 432; Suppl. I, 771.

16 (a) **Or. 1008 (9)**

1. *Qawānīn ḥikam al-ishrāq ilā kull al-Ṣūfīya bi-jamī' al-āfāq*, by Jamāl al-Dīn Abu 'l-Mawāhib Muḥammad b. Aḥmad Ibn Zaghdūn al-Tūnisī al-Wafā'ī al-Shādhilī (d. 822/1477). Ff. 3–42. Brockelmann, Suppl. II, 152.

2. *Nafaḥāt al-ṣafā' bi'l-sūl li-sharḥ Muqaddimāt al-uṣūl*, by Burhān al-Dīn Ibrāhīm b. Maḥmūd al-Aqsarā'ī al-Mawāhibī. (d. 908/1502). Ff. 43–90. Brockelmann, Suppl. II, 362.

Ff. 90. Clear scholar's naskh. 14 Sha'bān 1002/7 May 1594.

17 (a) **Or. 1009 (10)**

Sharḥ Kullīyāt al-Qānūn, by Quṭb al-Dīn Ibrāhīm b. 'Alī b. Muḥammad al-Sulamī al-Miṣrī (d. 618/1221).

Ff. 185. Clear scholar's naskh. Rabī' I 678/July 1279. Brockelmann, I, 457; Suppl. I, 824.

18 (a) **Or. 1010 (9)**

Mūjiz al-'ibārāt fī sharḥ alfāẓ al-Maqāmāt (vol. II), by Tāj al-Dīn Abū Ṭālib 'Alī b. Anjab b. 'Ubaid Allāh Ibn al-Sā'ī al-Khāzin al-Baghdādī (d. 674/1275).

Ff. 156. Excellent old vocalized naskh. Rajab 649/September 1251. Illuminated title-page. No other copy appears to be recorded.

19 (a) **Or. 1011 (8)**

Sharḥ (*Ḥall mushkilāt*) *al-Ishārāt wa'l-tanbīhāt*, by Nāṣir al-Dīn Muḥammad b. Muḥammad b. al-Ḥasan al-Ṭūsī (d. 672/1274).

Ff. 147. Scholar's ta'līq. Ramaḍān 760/Aug. 1359. Printed at Istanbul, 1290/1873; Teheran, 1301/1883, 1887; in India, 1281/1864, 1318/1900. Brockelmann I, 454; Suppl. I, 816.

20 (a) **Or. 1012 (9)**

Sharḥ al-Urjūza fī 'l-ṭibb, by Abu 'l-Walīd Muḥammad b. Aḥmad Ibn Rushd (d. 595/1198).

Ff. 117. Scholar's maghribī. Muḥarram 1129/Dec. 1716. Brockelmann, Suppl. I, 819.

21 (a) **Or. 1013 (8)**

Al-Shifā', by Abū 'Alī al-Ḥusain b. 'Abd Allāh Ibn Sīnā al-Qānūnī (d. 428/1037).

Ff. 110. Clear, unpointed naskh. 7/13th century. Brockelmann I, 454; Suppl. I, 815.

22 (a) **Or. 1014 (9)**

Ḍiyā' al-qulūb (*sharḥ Jilā' al-qulūb*), by Isḥāq b. Ḥasan al-Zanjānī al-Tuqātī (fl. 1095/1684).

Ff. 114. Scholar's ta'līq. 1107/1695–6. Brockelmann II, 440; Suppl. II, 654.

23 (a) **Or. 1015** (9)

'Uqūd al-jumān fī manāqib al-Imām Abī Ḥanīfa al-Nu'mān, by Shams al-Dīn Abū 'Abd Allāh Muḥammad b. Yūsuf b. 'Alī b. Yūsuf al-Dimashqī al-Ṣāliḥī al-Shāfi'ī al-Sha'mī (d. 942/1535).

Ff. 147. Scholar's naskh. Ṣafar 981/June 1573 (date of collation). Brockelmann II, 304; Suppl. II, 416.

24 (a) **Or. 1016** (9)

Al-Farā'id al-durrīya min al-jawāhir al-'Uṣfūrīya, by Abu'l-Ḍiyā' 'Alī b. Ibrāhīm b. Aḥmad al-Būtījī al-Shāfi'ī al-Ash'arī al-Aḥmadī al-Shādhilī (fl. 1100/1688).

Ff. 33. Scholar's cursive naskh. 15 Shauwāl 1107/19 May 1696. Autograph. No other copy appears to be recorded.

25 (a) **Or. 1017** (9)

Zād al-murīd lil-safar al-ba'īd.

Ff. 96. Scholar's naskh. 23 Muḥarram 1018/29 April 1609. Apparently autograph. No other copy appears to be recorded.

26 (a) **Or. 1018** (9)

Kāmil al-ṣinā'atain (or *Kāshif al-wail fī ma'rifat amrāḍ al-khail*), by Abū Bakr b. al-Mundhir al-Baiṭār (d. 741/1340).

Ff. 139. Clear naskh. Mid-Rabī' I 1121/end of May 1709. Translated into French by M. Perron (Paris, 1852–60). Brockelmann II, 136–7; Suppl. III, 1260.

27 (a) **Or. 1019** (11)

Kifāyat al-akhyār, by Taqī al-Dīn Abū Bakr b. Muḥammad b. 'Abd al-Mu'min al-Ḥiṣnī al-Shāfi'ī al-Dimashqī (d. 829/1426).

Ff. 181. Scholar's naskh. 27 Rabī' I 893/12 Mar. 1488. Printed at Cairo, 1350/1931. Brockelmann I, 392; Suppl. I, 677.

28 (p) **Or. 1020** (12)

Majālis al-mu'minīn, by Nūr Allāh b. Sharīf al-Ḥusainī al-Shūshtarī (fl. 1000/1598).

Ff. 499. Excellent nasta'līq. Undated, 11/17th century. Fine decorated sarlauḥ and 'unwān, gold and blue margins throughout. Lithographed several times. Ivanow-Curzon 276.

29 (a) **Or. 1021 (12)**

1. *Ṭibb al-fuqarā' wa'l-masākīn*, by Abū Ja'far Aḥmad b. Ibrāhīm b. Abī Khālid Ibn al-Jazzār (d. 395/1004). Ff. 1–26. Brockelmann I, 238.

2. *Tafsīr al-buqūl 'ala 'khtilāf al-ṭabā'i' wa'l-azmina.* Ff. 27*a*–29*b*[10]. No other copy appears to be recorded.

3. *Ṭibb al-'Ajam.* Ff. 29*b*[11]–35. No other copy appears to be recorded.

4. *Al-Ṭibb al-nabawī*, by Abū 'Abd Allāh Muḥammad b. Yūsuf b. 'Umar al-Ḥasanī al-Sanūsī (d. 892/1486). Ff. 36–41. Brockelmann II, 252; Suppl. II, 356.

5. *Al-Adwiyat al-mufrada*, by Abu'l-Ṣalt Umaiya b. Abi 'l-Ṣalt b. 'Abd al-'Azīz al-Andalusī (d. 529/1134). Ff. 42–70. Brockelmann I, 486; Suppl. I, 889.

6. *Al-Kāfiya fi 'l-ta'rīf bi'l-Hārūnīya*, by Masīḥ b. Ḥakīm al-Dimashqī. Ff. 71–116. Brockelmann, Suppl. II, 1029.

Ff. 116. Maghribī. 1121/1709–10.

30 (a) **Or. 1022 (9)**

Majmū' min aqwāl Jālīnūs wa-Abqirāṭ fī tadbīr al-nāqa wa-man shābahah min al-mahzūlīn.

Ff. 19. Excellent naskh. 24 Kānūn I/24 December 1751. No other copy appears to be recorded.

31 (a) **Or. 1023 (7)**

1. *Al-Mukhtaṣar fi 'l-ṭibb*, ascribed to Isḥāq b. Ḥunain (d. 298/910 or 299/911). Ff. 2–28. No other copy appears to be recorded.

2. *Al-Qaul al-sadīd fi 'khtiyār al-imā' wa'l-'abīd*, by Muẓaffar al-Dīn Abu 'l-Thanā' Maḥmūd b. Aḥmad al-'Aintābī al-Amshāṭī (d. 902/1496). Ff. 29–49. Brockelmann II, 82; Suppl. II, 93, 169.

Ff. 50. Two clear naskh hands: (1) 10/16th century; (2) 10 Rabī' II 964/10 Feb. 1557.

32 (a) **Or. 1024 (9)**

Al-Miṣbāḥ al-hādī ila 'l-salāma wa'l-najāḥ, by Badr al-Dīn Muḥammad b. Muḥammad al-Qauṣūnī (fl. 950/1543).

Ff. 20. Clear naskh. 10/16th century. Perhaps autograph. No other copy appears to be recorded.

33 (p) **Or. 1025 (8)**

Subḥat al-abrār, by Nūr al-Dīn 'Abd al-Rahmān b. Aḥmad Jāmī (d. 898/1494).

Ff. 112. Calligraphic nasta'līq. 10/16th century. Illuminated 'unwān, margins ruled throughout in gold and colours. Printed and lithographed several times. Ivanow 612 (20).

34 (p) **Or. 1026 (10)**

Abwāb al-jinān (ch. 1), by Muḥammad Rafī' Wā'iẓ Qazwīnī (d. *ca.* 1105/1694).

Ff. 396. Excellent nasta'līq. Rabī' 1 1089/April 1678. Fine decorated 'unwān, gilt margins throughout. Ivanow 1395.

35 (p) **Or. 1027 (11)**

Mathnawī-yi ma'nawī, by Jalāl al-Dīn Muḥammad b. Muḥammad Rūmī (d. 672/1273).

Ff. 384. Excellent nasta'līq. 1040/1630–1. Decorated 'unwāns, margins in gilt and colours throughout. Lithographed and printed many times. Ivanow 490.

36 (p) **Or. 1031 (7)**

Qaṣīda [in honour of Queen Victoria], by Mīrzā Muḥammad Bāqir Bawānātī called Ibrāhīm Jān Mu'aṭṭar (d. *ca.* 1890).

Ff. 12. Good nasta'līq, presumably holograph. December 1876. Presented by the Executors of Miss Adelaide Manning.

37 (p) **Or. 1032 (13)**

Karīmā (*Pand-nāma*), attributed to Musharrif al-Dīn Muṣliḥ b. 'Abd Allāh Sa'dī (d. 691/1292).

Ff. 12. Good nasta'līq. 12/18th century. Illuminated 'unwān; four miniature paintings. Often lithographed and printed. Ivanow 543. Presented by Mr J. E. de C. Davy.

38 (p) **Or. 1036 (13)**

Mathnawī-yi ma'nawī (daftars IV–VI), by Rūmī. *See* no. 35.

Ff. 224. Excellent calligraphic nasta'līq. Ramaḍān 994/August 1586. Fine illuminated 'unwāns, margins ruled throughout in gold and colours. Lacquer binding.

39 (a) **Or. 1037 (23)**

Mu'āhadat al-ḥimāya wa'l-mawadda. [Draft of a Treaty between Germany and an unspecified Arab ruler.]

Fol. 1. Calligraphic naskh. Undated, early 14/20th century. Presented by Capt. Haseldon.

40 (p) **Or. 1038 (11)**

Dīwān, by Shams al-Dīn Muḥammad Ḥāfiẓ Shīrāzī (d. 791/1389).

Ff. 180. Good nasta'līq. 16 Ramaḍān 1080/17 Jan. 1670. Printed and lithographed frequently. Ivanow 587. Francis Jenkinson bequest.

41 (p) **Or. 1041 (7)**

Lubāb al-ḥisāb fī 'ilm al-turāb.

Ff. 48. Fine old naskh. 7/13th century.

42 (a) **Or. 1042 (8)**

Qur'ān.

Ff. 359. Excellent naskh. 10/16th century. Fine double-page illuminated frontispiece and 'unwān, marginal ornaments. Seal of 'Ālamgīr (Aurangzeb) dated 1115/1703 and later Moghul emperors. Presented by Walter Sibbald Adie, M.A., I.C.S. (1924).

43 (a) **Or. 1043 (8)**

Qur'ān.

Ff. 397. Good vocalized Indian naskh. 13 Ṣafar 1120/4 May 1708. Margins ruled in red, blue and yellow. Presented by W. S. Adie.

44 (a) **Or. 1044 (11)**

Qur'ān (with interlineary Persian translation).

Ff. 301. Calligraphic naskh and nasta'līq. 1011/1602–3. Fully illuminated double opening, gilt margins and clouds throughout. Presented by W. S. Adie.

45 (a) **Or. 1045 (11)**

Qur'ān (with Persian interlineary translation).

Ff. 239. Calligraphic naskh and nasta'līq. Undated, 11/17th century. Three finely illuminated double openings, gilt margins and marginal ornaments throughout. Presented by W. S. Adie.

46 (a) **Or. 1046** (9)

1. *Takhmīs al-Burda*. Ff. 1–30.

2. *Aṭbāq al-dhahab*, by 'Abd al-Mu'min b. Hibat Allāh al-Maghribi al-Iṣfahānī Shufurwa (fl. 600/1203). Ff. 33–101. Printed several times. Brockelmann I, 292; Suppl. I, 512.

Ff. 102. Clear vocalized naskh. 11/17th century. Presented by W. S. Adie.

47 (a) **Or. 1047** (8)

Ghurar al-ḥikam wa-durar al-kalim, attributed to 'Alī b. Abī Ṭālib, Caliph (edited by 'Abd al-Wāḥid b. Muḥammad b. 'Abd al-Wāḥid al-Āmidī al-Tamīmī (d. 436/1044)).

Ff. 229. Excellent naskh. 11/17th century. Gilt margins ruled. Lithographed at Bombay 1280/1863. Brockelmann I, 44; Suppl. I, 75. Presented by W. S. Adie.

48 (a) **Or. 1048** (9)

Al-Ṣaḥīfat al-kāmila, attributed to Zain al-'Ābidīn 'Alī b. al-Ḥusain (d. 92/710).

Ff. 113. Good large vocalized naskh. 12/18th century. First opening fully illuminated; gilt margins. Often printed and lithographed. Brockelmann I, 44; Suppl. I, 76. Presented by W. S. Adie.

49 (a) **Or. 1049** (10)

Al-Istibṣār fīmā 'khtulifa fīhi min al-akhbār, by Abū Ja'far Muḥammad b. al-Ḥasan al-Ṭūsī (d. 459/1067).

Ff. 242. Clear naskh. Tuesday 9 Rajab 1072/28 Feb. 1662. Margins ruled throughout in gold and black. Printed several times. Brockelmann I, 405, Suppl. I, 707. Presented by W. S. Adie.

50 (p) **Or. 1050** (11), **1051** (11)

Minhāj al-ṣādiqīn fī ilzām al-mukhālifīn (vols. I and II), by Fatḥ Allāh b. Shukr Allāh al-Sharīf al-Kāshānī (d. *ca.* 990/1582–3).

Foliation impracticable. Good naskh. 12/18th century. Illuminated 'unwān, margins ruled throughout in gold and colours. Printed twice in Persia. Storey, p. 15, no. 23 (1). Presented by W. S. Adie.

51 (p) **Or. 1052 (12)**

Tarjuma-yi Quṭbshāhī-yi Aḥādīth-i arbaʻīn, by Bahā' al-Dīn Muḥammad b. Ḥusain b. ʻAbd al-Ṣamad al-ʻĀmilī al-Bahā'ī (d. 1030/1621).

Ff. 295. Excellent nastaʻlīq. 1029/1620. Brockelmann, Suppl. II, 595. Presented by W. S. Adie.

52 (p) **Or. 1053 (12)**

ʻAin al-ḥayāt, by Muḥammad Bāqir b. Muḥammad Taqī Majlisī (d. *ca.* 1111/1700).

Ff. 395. Variable nastaʻlīq. 5 Rajab 1136/30 March 1724. Printed at Teheran, 1240/1825. Ethé, I.O. 2668. Presented by W. S. Adie.

53 (p) **Or. 1054 (12)**

Zād al-maʻād, by Muḥammad Bāqir b. Muḥammad Taqī Majlisī.

Ff. 301. Excellent naskh. 1222/1807. Fol. 1*b*–2*a* richly illuminated, gold and turquoise margins and gold clouds throughout. Often lithographed. Ivanow 1121. Presented by W. S. Adie.

54 (p) **Or. 1055 (10)**

Zād al-maʻād. Another copy.

Ff. 338. Excellent naskh. Ramaḍān 1107/April 1696. Fine decorated ʻunwān, margins throughout in gold and colours. Holograph of author. Presented by W. S. Adie.

55 (p) **Or. 1056 (10)**

Zād al-maʻād. Another copy.

Ff. 391. Excellent naskh. 12/18th century. Decorated ʻunwān, margins throughout in gold, red and black. Presented by W. S. Adie.

56 (p) **Or. 1057 (13)**

Zād al-maʻād. Another copy.

Ff. 325. Clear naskh and nastaʻlīq. 17 Rabīʻ II 1238/1 Jan. 1823. Illuminated opening page, margins ruled in gold and colours throughout. Presented by W. S. Adie.

57 (p) **Or. 1058** (12)

Baḥr al-bukā', by Muḥammad b. Muḥammad Ṣādiq Shūshtarī.

Ff. 346. Clear nasta'līq. 12/18th century. Presented by W. S. Adie.

58 (p) **Or. 1059** (11)

Sawāniḥ-i Dakan, by Mun'im Khān b. 'Abd al-Mughnī Hamadhānī Aurangābādī (fl. 1197/1783).

Ff. 202. Calligraphic nasta'līq. 1229/1814. Illuminated 'unwān, margins ruled throughout in gold and colours. Storey, p. 749, no. 1030. Presented by W. S. Adie.

59 (p) **Or. 1060** (9)

Shigarf-nāma-yi wilāyat, by I'tiṣām al-Dīn b. Tāj al-Dīn Pājnūrī (fl. 1180/1766).

Ff. 115. Clear nasta'līq. 8 Rajab 1222/11 Sept. 1807. Ivanow-Curzon 96. Presented by W. S. Adie.

60 (p) **Or. 1061** (9)

Kāmil al-ta'bīr, by Abu'l-Faḍl Ḥusain b. Ibrāhīm b. Muḥammad Tiflīsī (fl. 6/12th century).

Ff. 267. Clear naskh. 10/16th century. Fully illuminated opening pages and 'unwān; margins ruled throughout in gold and black. Ivanow 1508. Presented by W. S. Adie.

61 (p) **Or. 1062** (11)

Tarjamat al-Faraj ba'd al-shidda, by Ḥusain b. As'ad Dihistānī Mu'aiyadī (fl. 6/12th century).

Ff. 194. Excellent nasta'līq. Rabī' II 1066/Jan. 1656. Margins ruled in gold and blue throughout. Ivanow 296. Presented by W. S. Adie.

62 (p) **Or. 1063** (8)

Būstān, by Sa'dī.

Ff. 145. Excellent nasta'līq. 1205/1790–1. Illuminated 'unwān, margins ruled throughout in gold and black. Often printed and lithographed. Ivanow 529. Presented by W. S. Adie.

63 (p) **Or. 1064 (13)**

Mathnawī-yi ma'nawī, by Rūmī. *See* no. 35.

Ff. 276. Excellent nasta'līq. 10/16th century. Illuminated 'unwāns, margins ruled throughout in gold and colours. Presented by W. S. Adie.

64 (p) **Or. 1065 (8)**

Nairang-i 'ishq, by Muḥammad Akram Panjābī called Ghanīmat (d. *ca.* 1100/1698).

Ff. 97. Good nasta'līq. 12/18th century. Lithographed several times in India. Ivanow 819. Presented by W. S. Adie.

65 (p) **Or. 1066 (9)**

Rasā'il, by Mullā Ṭughrā Mashhadī (d. *ca.* 1078/1667).

Ff. 191. Clear nasta'līq. 12/18th century. Lithographed several times. Ivanow 371. Presented by W. S. Adie.

66 (p) **Or. 1067 (9)**

Three untitled treatises in prose.

Ff. 291. Clear Indian nasta'līq. 12/18th century. Presented by W. S. Adie.

67 (p) **Or. 1068 (9)**

1. *Mukhtaṣar dar bayān-i wājibāt-i namāz*, by Ḍiyā' al-Dīn al-Jurjānī. Ff. 1–104.

2. A versified tract on Law, by Ḥāfiẓī. Ff. 105–114.

3. *Anwār al-sarā'ir wa-miṣbāḥ al-zā'ir*. Ff. 115–154.

4. *Risāla*, by Yuḥannā b. 'Abd al-Karīm Ḥaidarī. Ff. 155–171 *a*.

5. *Sharḥ-i Chahārdah ḥadīth*, by Muḥammad Bāqir b. Muḥammad Taqī Majlisī (d. *ca.* 1111/1700). Ff. 171 *b*–268. Ivanow 1119 (1).

6. *Risāla dar qiyāfa*. Ff. 269–302.

Ff. 302. Clear nasta'līq. 12/18th century. Presented by W. S. Adie.

68 (p) **Or. 1069 (11)**

1. *Fawā'id-i khamsa*, by Dīdār 'Alī 'Aẓīmābādī.

2. *Chahār gulzār*, and other tracts.

Ff. 191. Good nasta'līq. 1247/1831–2. Presented by W. S. Adie.

69 (p) **Or. 1070 (9)**

A collection of model letters, incomplete at the beginning.

Ff. 118. Clear nasta'līq. 12/18th century. Presented by W. S. Adie.

70 (p) **Or. 1071 (9)**

Qiṣṣa-yi Fīrūzshāh.

Ff. 50. Clear nasta'līq. 12/18th century. Ethé, I.O. 803 (1). Presented by W. S. Adie.

71 (p) **Or. 1072 (14)**

Burhān-i qāṭi', by Muḥammad Ḥusain b. Khalaf Tabrīzī called Burhān (fl. 1062/1652).

Ff. 278. Good nasta'līq. 20 Jumādā II 1237/15 March 1822. Margins ruled in colours throughout. Printed several times. Ivanow 1426. Presented by W. S. Adie.

72 (p) **Or. 1073 (9)**

A dictionary of medicine, untitled and lacking the beginning.

Ff. 190. Clear nasta'līq. 11/17th century. Presented by W. S. Adie.

73 (p) **Or. 1074 (9)**

A fragment of a treatise on medicine.

Ff. 276. Clear nasta'līq. 11/17th century. Presented by W. S. Adie.

74 (p) **Or. 1075 (9)**

An anonymous collection of medical prescriptions.

Ff. 191. Clear Indian nasta'līq. 12/18th century. Presented by W. S. Adie.

75 (a, p) **Or. 1087 (11)**

Ṣad kalima, attributed to 'Alī b. Abī Ṭālib, with interlineary Persian verse translation.

Ff. 18. Excellent calligraphic naskh. 10/16th century. Illuminated 'unwān, margins ruled in gold and colours with floral sprays throughout. Printed several times. Brockelmann, Suppl. I, 75. Presented by Mrs C. H. H. Macartney (1925).

76 (a) **Or. 1088** (9)

Fatḥ al-qarīb al-mujīb fī sharḥ alfāẓ al-Taqrīb (or, *al-Qaul al-mukhtār fī sharḥ Ghāyat al-ikhtiṣār*), by Muḥammad b. al-Qāsim al-Ghazzī (d. 918/1512).

Ff. 109. Clear naskh. 11/17th century. Frequently printed. Brockelmann I, 392; Suppl. I, 677. Presented by Mrs Macartney.

77 (a) **Or. 1089** (7)

Fragments of two separate works.

Ff. 168. Indian naskh and nasta'līq. 14 Shauwal 1026/15 Oct. 1617. Presented by Mrs Macartney.

78 (a) **Or. 1090** (7)

Qaṣīdat al-Burda, by Sharaf al-Dīn Abū 'Abd Allāh Muḥammad b. Sa'īd al-Būṣīrī al-Ṣanhājī (d. 694/1296).

Ff. 19. Excellent calligraphic thulth and naskh. 8/14th century. Gilt and black margins. Often printed. Brockelmann I, 265; Suppl. I, 467. Presented by Mrs Macartney.

79 (a) **Or. 1091** (7)

Al-Qusṭās fi 'l-'arūḍ, by Abu 'l-Qāsim Maḥmūd b. 'Umar al-Zamakhsharī (d. 538/1144).

Ff. 22. Clear scholar's naskh. 7/13th century. Brockelmann I, 291; Suppl. I, 511. Presented by Mrs Macartney.

80 (a) **Or. 1092** (8)

Al-Qustās fi 'l-'arūḍ. An annotated transcription by C. H. H. Macartney of no. 79.

Ff. 45. European hand. 20th century. Presented by Mrs Macartney.

81 (a) **Or. 1093** (10)

Al-Qusṭās fi 'l-'arūḍ. A second annotated transcription by C. H. H. Macartney of no. 79.

Ff. 36. European hand. 20th century. Presented by Mrs Macartney.

82 (a) **Or. 1094** (10)

Al-Qusṭās fi 'l-'arūḍ. A third transcription of no. 79 by C. H. H. Macartney in the form of an edition.

Ff. 29. European hand. 20th century. Presented by Mrs Macartney.

83 (a) **Or. 1095** (10)

Translation of the *Dīwān* of Dhu 'l-Rumma, by C. H. H. Macartney.

Ff. 187. English cursive hand, *ca.* 1910. *See* Brockelmann, Suppl. I, 89. Presented by Mrs Macartney.

84 (a) **Or. 1096** (9)

Glossary to the *Kitāb al-Aghānī*, by C. H. H. Macartney.

Ff. 193. European hand. Early 20th century. Presented by Mrs Macartney.

85 (a) **Or. 1097** (9)

Notes on the *Dīwān* of Dhu 'l-Rumma, by C. H. H. Macartney.

Ff. 86. European hand. Early 20th century. Presented by Mrs Macartney.

86 (a) **Or. 1098** (9)

Notes on the *Dīwān* of Dhu 'l-Rumma, by C. H. H. Macartney.

Ff. 95. European hand. Early 20th century. Presented by Mrs Macartney.

87 (a) **Or. 1099** (9)

Notes on the *Dīwān* of Dhu 'l-Rumma, by C. H. H. Macartney.

Ff. 88. European hand. Early 20th century. Presented by Mrs Macartney.

88 (a) **Or. 1100** (9)

Miscellaneous notes, by C. H. H. Macartney and F. Krenkow.

Ff. 98. European hands. Early 20th century. Presented by Mrs Macartney.

89 (p) **Or. 1150–1** (7)

Baṣīrat al-abṣār (extract from), followed by a tract in Sindhi.

Ff. 32. Clear nasta'līq and naskh. 27 October 1883. Presented by W. Heffer and Sons Ltd.

90 (p) **Or. 1154** (9)

1. *Ma'dan al-ḥisāb*, by Bīm Rāj, Ff. 1–136. (Formerly Lee 161[1].)

2. *Muntakhab Khulāṣat al-ḥisāb*, by Luṭf Allāh Muhandis b. Aḥmad Mi'mār Lāhūrī.

Ff. 173. Clear nasta'līq. Late 12/18th century. Ethé, I.O. 2253.

91 (p) **Or. 1155** (9)

Risāla fi 'l-hai'a, by 'Alā' al-Dīn 'Alī b. Muḥammad al-Qūshjī (d. 879/1474).

Ff. 52. Calligraphic nasta'līq. 10/16th century. Geometrical and astronomical drawings. Margins ruled. Ivanow 1489.

92 (p) **Or. 1156** (8)

Līlāvatī of Bhāskara Ācārya, translated into Persian by Abu 'l-Faiḍ b. Mubārak Nāgūrī, called Faiḍī (d. 1004/1595).

Ff. 88. Cursive ta'līq. 20 Dhu 'l-Ḥijja 1212/5 June 1798. Margins ruled. Printed at Calcutta, 1827. Ivanow 1694.

93 (a) **Or. 1164** (5)

A collection of Muslim litanies and prayers.

Ff. 220. West African hand. 14/20th century.

94 (p) **Or. 1184** (9)

Nafaḥāt al-uns, by Jāmī (d. 898/1492).

Ff. 313. Excellent nasta'līq. 10/16th century. Margins ruled in gilt and blue. Often printed. Ivanow 248.

95 (p) **Or. 1185** (9)

Index to the *Nafaḥāt al-uns* of Jāmī, compiled by Clément Huart.

Ff. 8. European hand. Early 20th century.

96 (a) **Or. 1186** (9)

'Uyūn al-akhbār wa-funūn al-āthār fī dhikr al-Nabī al-Muṣṭafā 'l-mukhtār (vol. II), by 'Imād al-Dīn Idrīs b. al-Ḥasan b. 'Abd Allāh al-Makramī (d. 872/1368).

Ff. 241. Clear naskh. 16 Jumādā II 1351/17 Sept. 1932. Brockelmann, Suppl. II, 250.

97 (a) **Or. 1187** (9)

'Uyūn al-akhbār wa-funūn al-āthār fī dhikr al-Nabī al-Muṣṭafā 'l-mukhtār (vol. III).

Ff. 252. Clear naskh. 14/20th century.

98 (a) **Or. 1188** (9)

'Uyūn al-akhbār wa-funūn al-āthār fī dhikr al-Nabī al-Muṣṭafā 'l-mukhtār (vol. VII).

Ff. 242. Clear naskh. 4 Jumādā I 1350/17 Oct. 1931.

99 (a) **Or. 1190** (12)

Zād al-ma'ād, by Muḥammad Bāqir. *See* no. 53.

Ff. 400. Calligraphic naskh. Rajab 1271/March 1855. Elaborate 'unwān, margins ruled in gold and black.

100 (a) **Or. 1191** (8)

Qur'ān.

Ff. 359. Calligraphic naskh. 11 Dhu 'l-Qa'da 1204/23 July 1790. Illuminated opening and concluding pages; margins ruled in green, gilt and blue. Presented by Arthur William Young, M.A. (1933).

101 (a) **Or. 1192** (8)

Al-Faṣīḥ, by Abu 'l-'Abbās Aḥmad b. Yaḥyā called Tha'lab (d. 291/904).

Ff. 43. Clear vocalized naskh. Jumādā I 573/Oct.–Nov. 1177. Frequently printed with commentary. Brockelmann I, 118; Suppl. I, 181.

102 (a) **Or. 1225** (11)

Al-Dhakhīra fī maḥāsin ahl al-Jazīra, by Abu 'l-Ḥasan 'Alī b. Bassām al-Shantarīnī (d. 543/1147), (vols. II–III).

Ff. 317. Clear maghribī. 12/18th century. Printed at Cairo, 1939–. Brockelmann I, 339; Suppl. I, 579.

103 (a) **Or. 1229** (8)

Fatḥ al-Raḥmān bi-kashf mā yalbas fi 'l-Qur'ān, by Zain al-Dīn Abū Yaḥyā Zakarīyā' b. Muḥammad Ibn al-Anṣārī al-Sumaikī al-Shāfi'ī (d. 926/1521).

Ff. 100. Clear scholar's naskh. 10/16th century. Printed at Bulaq, 1299/1882. Brockelmann II, 99; Suppl. II, 118.

104 (t) **Or. 1230** (8)

Wāmiq u 'Udhrā, by Maḥmūd b. 'Uthmān b. 'Alī al-Naqqāsh Lāmi'ī (d. 938/1532 or 940/1534).

Ff. 186. Good nasta'līq. 933/1526–7. Translated by von Hammer, Vienna, 1833.

105 (a) **Or. 1231** (7)

Sharḥ Qaṣīdat al-Bustī al-nūnīya, by 'Abd Allāh b. Muḥammad b. Aḥmad al-Nuqrakār (d. 776/1374).

Ff. 55. Excellent naskh. 9/15th century. Brockelmann I, 251; Suppl. I, 445.

106 (a) **Or. 1232** (9)

Al-Milal wa'l-niḥal (first half), by Abu'l-Fatḥ Muḥammad b. 'Abd al-Karīm al-Shahrastānī (d. 548/1153).

Ff. 189. Clear naskh. 8/14th century. Printed several times. Brockelmann I, 428; Suppl. I, 762–3.

107 (p) **Or. 1233** (12)

1. *Maktūbāt*, vol. III, by Aḥmad Fārūqī Sirhindī, called Imām-i Rabbānī (d. 1034/1624). Ff. 1–128. Lithographed several times in India. Ivanow 1268.

2. *Maktūbāt*, vol. II, by Muḥammad Ma'ṣūm b. Aḥmad Fārūqī (d. 1080/1669). Ff. 129–272. Lithographed at Amritsar, 1340/1922. Bankipore 1394.

Ff. 272. Clear naskh. 11 Dhu 'l-Qa'da 1150/2 March 1738. Margins ruled in red.

108 (p) **Or. 1234** (12)

Safar-nāma, by Muḥammad Sajjād 'Alī Khān, called Auj.

Ff. 47. Excellent nasta'līq. 28 Jumādā I 1301/27 March 1884.

109 (p) **Or. 1235** (11)

Hasht bihisht (vol. VI), by Idrīs b. Ḥusām al-Dīn 'Alī Bidlīsī (d. 926/1520).

Ff. 150. Clear nasta'līq. 1093/1682. Storey, p. 412, no. 587.

110 (a) **Or. 1236** (11)

Al-Yawāqīt fī 'ilm al-mawāqīt, by Ibrāhīm b. 'Alī b. Muḥammad al-Janadī.

Ff. 56. Excellent naskh. 10/16th century. Decorated sarlauḥ and 'unwān, margins in gold, blue and black throughout. Apparently author's holograph. No other copy appears to be recorded.

111 (a) **Or. 1237 (11)**

Al-Jauhar al-maṣūn fī 'ulūm kitāb Allāh al-maknūn, by Abu'l-Mawāhib 'Abd al-Wahhāb b. Aḥmad al-Sha'rānī al-Shāfi'ī (d. 973/1565).

Ff. 77. Good scholar's naskh. 10/16th century. Brockelmann II, 338; Suppl. II, 466.

112 (a) **Or. 1238 (10)**

Ta'bīr al-ru'yā, by Abu'l-Ṭāhir Ibrāhīm b. Yaḥyā b. Ghannām al-Ḥarrāni al-Numairī al-Ḥanbalī al-Maqdisī (d. 674/1275 or 693/1294).

Ff. 106. Clear naskh. 8/14th century. Brockelmann I, 498; Suppl. I, 913.

113 (p) **Or. 1239 (10)**

Badā'i' al-afkār fī ṣanā'i' al-ash'ār, by Ḥusain b. 'Alī al-Wā'iẓ al-Kāshifī (d. 910/1504).

Ff. 41. Clear ta'līq. Rabī' I 1162/Feb. 1749. Coloured 'unwān; gilt borders throughout. Browne, Cambridge Cat. CLXXX.

114 (p) **Or. 1240 (9)**

Dīwān, by Muḥammad-Qulī Salīm Ṭihrānī (d. 1057/1647).

Ff. 73. Clear nīm-shikasta. 12/18th century. Bankipore 311, Ivanow 748.

115 (p) **Or. 1242 (9)**

Dīwān, by Nāẓim.

Ff. 48. Clear nasta'līq. 1243/1827–8. Browne 248.

116 (p) **Or. 1243 (9)**

Siyāḥat-nāma-yi Khīwā, by Riḍā-Qulī Khān Hidāyat (d. 1288/1870).

Ff. 55. Excellent nasta'līq. 13/19th century. Margins ruled in red and blue. Printed at Paris [Cairo], 1876 s.t. 'Rélation de l'Ambassade au Kharezm (Khiva) de Riza Qouly Khan'.

117 (p) **Or. 1244 (9)**

Dīwān, by Shams al-Dīn Ḥabīb Allāh Mīrzā Jānjānān Maẓhar (d. 1195/1781).

Ff. 49. Clear nasta'līq. 12/18th century. Margins ruled in red and blue. Lithographed several times in India. Ivanow 875.

118 (a) **Or. 1245** (8)

Al-Shifā' (*al-Ilāhīyāt*), by Abū 'Alī al-Ḥusain b. 'Abd Allāh Ibn Sīnā (d. 428/1037). *See* no. 21.

Ff. 167. Clear naskh. Rabī' I 1074/Oct. 1663.

119 (p, t) **Or. 1246** (8)

Dīwān, by Nuṣrat (fl. 1170/1756).

Ff. 67. Good nasta'līq. Late 12/18th century. Coloured 'unwān and gold borders throughout.

120 (a) **Or. 1247** (8)

Al-Jawāhir al-khamsa, by Abu'l-Mu'aiyad Muḥammad b. Khaṭīr al-Dīn b. Bāyazīd al-Ghauth al-Hindī (d. 970/1562).

Ff. 227. Scholar's naskh. 23 Jumādā II 1042/5 Jan. 1633. Printed at Fez, 1318/1900–1. Brockelmann II, 418; Suppl. II, 616.

121 (a) **Or. 1248** (8)

Ḥikāya Jardāmah b. Shāhin-Shāh.

Ff. 167. Clear naskh. Tuesday, 29 Shauwāl 857/2 Nov. 1453.

122 (a) **Or. 1249** (8)

Al-Arba'īn fī uṣūl al-dīn, by Abū Ḥāmid Muḥammad b. Muḥammad al-Ghazālī (d. 505/1111).

Ff. 212. Excellent old naskh. Saturday, 13 Dhu 'l-Ḥijja 505/11 June 1112. Printed frequently. Brockelmann I, 421; Suppl. I, 746.

123 (a) **Or. 1250** (8)

Ṭirāz al-majālis, by Shihāb al-Dīn Aḥmad b. Muḥammad b. 'Umar al-Khafājī (d. 1069/1659).

Ff. 201. Excellent naskh. Thursday, 27 Rajab 1124/30 Aug. 1712. Gilt 'unwān, red margins ruled. Printed at Cairo, 1284/1867, [1907]. Brockelmann II, 286; Suppl. II, 396.

124 (a) **Or. 1252** (8)

Nahj al-sulūk ilā naṣīḥat al-mulūk, by Aḥmad b. 'Abd al-Mun'im b. Khaiyām b. Yūsuf al-Damanhūrī al-Madhāhibī al-Azharī (d. 1192/1778).

Ff. 21. Excellent naskh. 1208/1793–4. Red margins ruled. No other copy appears to be recorded.

125 (a) **Or. 1253 (8)**

1. *Al-Ajwibat al-mufīda 'ala 'l-as'ilat al-'adīda*, by Najm al-Dīn Muḥammad b. Aḥmad b. 'Alī al-Ghaiṭī al-Iskandarī al-Shāfi'ī (d. 981/1573). Ff. 1–17*a*. Brockelmann II, 339; Suppl. II, 468.

1. *Nail al-marām fi 'l-ḥafaẓat al-kirām*, by Sharaf al-Dīn b. 'Abd al-Qādir Ibn Ḥabīb al-Ghazzī (d. 1005/1596). Ff. 17*b*–25. No other copy appears to be recorded.

Ff. 27. Excellent naskh. Monday, 14 Rajab 1148/30 Nov. 1735.

126 (a) **Or. 1254 (8)**

Irshād al-qāṣid ilā asna 'l-maqāṣid, by Shams al-Dīn Abū 'Abd Allāh Muḥammad b. Ibrāhīm b. Ṣā'id al-Sinjārī al-Miṣrī Ibn al-Akfānī al-Anṣārī (d. 749/1348).

Ff. 1–34. Excellent naskh. 1119/1707–8. Printed at Cairo, 1900. Brockelmann II, 136; Suppl. II, 169.

127 (a) **Or. 1255 (8)**

Itḥāf al-akhiṣṣā' bi-faḍā'il al-masjid al-aqṣā, by Shams al-Dīn Abū 'Abd Allāh Muḥammad b. Aḥmad b. 'Alī al-Minhājī al-Suyūṭī (d. *ca.* 880/1475). (Followed by various extracts, ff. 148–163.)

Ff. 35–147. Excellent naskh. 24 Rajab 1119/21 Oct. 1707. Brockelmann II, 133; Suppl. II, 164.

128 (a) **Or. 1256 (8)**

Nuzhat al-udabā' wa-salwat al-qurabā', by 'Umar al-Ḥalabī (fl. 1100/1688).

Ff. 163–224. Excellent naskh. 9 Rabī' I 1119/10 June 1707. Brockelmann, Suppl. II, 414.

129 (a) **Or. 1257 (8)**

Al-Siyāsat al-mulūkīya wa'l-akhlāq al-ikhtiyārīya, attributed to Plato.

Ff. 225–242. Excellent naskh. 8 Jumādā II 1118/18 Aug. 1706. Cf. Brockelmann, Suppl. I, 229.

130 (a) **Or. 1258 (8)**

Malḥama, attributed to Daniel. (Followed by scraps, ff. 259–65.)

Ff. 243–259. Excellent naskh. *ca.* 1119/1707–8. Cf. Ahlwardt 5912, 5915.

131 (a, t) **Or. 1259** (8)

Uṣūl al-ḥikam fī niẓām al-ʻālam, by Kāfī Ḥasan Efendī al-Āqḥiṣārī (d. 1025/1616), with Turkish paraphrase.

Ff. 46. Excellent naskh. 1182/1768–9. Illuminated ʻunwān. Brockelmann II, 443; Suppl. II, 659.

132 (a) **Or. 1260** (8)

Idrāk al-ḥaqīqa fī takhrīj aḥādīth al-Ṭarīqa, by ʻAlī b. al-Ḥasan al-Tamānī al-Ḥanafī al-Rifāʻī al-Māturīdī (fl. 1050/1640).

Ff. 121. Excellent taʻlīq. 17 Rajab 1057/18 Aug. 1647. Autograph. Brockelmann, Suppl. II, 656.

133 (a) **Or. 1261** (8)

Sharḥ al-Shajarat al-Nuʻmānīya fi'l-Daulat al-ʻUthmānīya, by Ṣadr al-Dīn Abu 'l-Maʻālī Muḥammad b. Isḥāq b. Muḥammad al-Qūnawī (d. 672/1273).

Ff. 96. Clear naskh. Friday, 21 Jumādā I 1074/21 Dec. 1663. Brockelmann I, 447; Suppl. I, 799.

134 (a) **Or. 1264** (8)

Sharḥ al-Nūnīya fi 'l-ʻaqā'id, by Aḥmad b. Mūsā al- Khayālī al-Chelebī (d. 863/1459).

Ff. 88. Excellent naskh. 10/16th century. Brockelmann, II, 229; Suppl. II, 321.

135 (p) **Or. 1265** (8)

1. *Munsha'āt*, by Jāmī (d. 898/1492). Ff. 1–59. Ivanow 612 (28). Printed at Calcutta, 1811, etc.

2. *Risāla-yi ḥūrā'īya*, by Jāmī (?). Ff. 60–62*a*. Ivanow 1239 (52).

3. *Risāla-yi ḥūrā'īya*, by Jalāl al-Dīn Muḥammad b. Asʻad al-Dawānī (d. 908/1503) (?). Ff. 62*b*–64; and other scraps. Ethé, I.O. 1919 (2).

Ff. 73. Clear taʻlīq. 10/16th century.

136 (a) **Or. 1267** (7)

Dīwān, by Fakhr al-Dīn Abū Bakr b. Muḥammad al-Ḥakkāk al-Ṣūfī (fl. 750/1349).

Ff. 150. Clear naskh. 11/17th century. Brockelmann II, 10; Suppl. II, 3.

137 (a) **Or. 1269 (7)**

Arba'ūn ḥadīthan, by Burhān al-Dīn Ibrāhīm b. 'Alī b. Aḥmad al-Qurashī al-Shāfi'ī Ibn al-Qalqashandī (d. 922/1516).

Ff. 30. Excellent vocalized naskh. Early 10/16th century. Author's autograph attestation dated 28 Ṣafar 911/1 August 1505 on ff. 23*b*–24*a*. No other copy appears to be recorded.

138 (a) **Or. 1270 (7)**

Ḥāshiya 'alā kitāb al-Talwīḥ, by Muḥammad b. Muḥammad b. Bilāl al-Ḥanafī al-Ḥalabī (d. 957/1550).

Ff. 66. Excellent naskh. 23 Dhu 'l-Ḥijja 933/20 Sept. 1527. Author's holograph copy. No other copy appears to be recorded.

139 (p) **Or. 1271 (7)**

Sharḥ Niṣāb al-ṣubyān, by Muḥammad b. Faṣīh b. Muḥammad called Karīm al-Dasht-bayāḍī (fl. 10/16th century).

Ff. 74. Nasta'līq. 12/18th century. Ivanow-Curzon 538.

140 (a) **Or. 1272 (7)**

Al-Kāfī fi 'l-farā'iḍ, by Abu Ya'qūb Isḥāq b. Ya'qūb b. 'Abd al-Ṣamad al-Ṣardafi al-Yamanī (d. 500/1106).

Ff. 208. Clear naskh. 9/15th century. Brockelmann I, 470; Suppl. I, 855.

141 (a) **Or. 1273 (7)**

Yatīmat al-dahr fī fatāwā ahl al-'aṣr, by 'Alā' al-Dīn 'Abd al-Raḥmān called al-Tarjumān (d. 645/1247).

Ff. 249. Clear naskh. 11/17th century. Decorated title-page and 'unwān; margins ruled in red. Brockelmann I, 381.

142 (p) **Or. 1274 (7)**

Dīwān, by Mu'īn al-Dīn 'Alī called Qāsim-i Anwār (d. 837/1433).

Ff. 216. Nasta'līq. 9/15th century. Ethé, I.O. 1285.

143 (p) **Or. 1275 (6)**

Dīwān-i Shams-i Tabrīz (selections), by Jalāl al-Dīn Rūmī (d. 672/1273).

Ff. 202. Excellent old naskh. 8/14th century. Lithographed frequently. Bankipore 87.

144 (p) **Or. 1276 (6)**

Dīwān, by Faḍl Allāh al-Ḥurūfī (d. 804/1402).

Ff. 189. Clear nasta'līq. 12/18th century.

145 (p) **Or. 1277 (5)**

A Ḥurūfī treatise.

Ff. 378. Good nasta'līq. 992/1584. Crude illuminated 'unwān; margins ruled in red. For another copy see *J.R.A.S.* 1907, p. 544 (Brit. Mus. Or. 5958).

146 (p) **Or. 1280 (7)**

Dastūr-i 'ushshāq, by Yaḥyā Sībak Fattāḥī (d. 852/1448).

Ff. 222. Excellent calligraphic nasta'līq. 885/1480. Richly illuminated double opening; seven miniatures in poor condition. Presented by R. S. Greenshields, who edited it in 1926.

147 (a) **Or. 1281 (10)**

Al-Risālā ila 'l-Ṣūfīya, by al-Qushairī (d. 465/1072). *See* no. 15.

Ff. 266. Excellent naskh. Jumādā I 561/March 1166.

148 (a) **Or. 1282 (7)**

Wujūh al-Qur'ān, by Abū 'Abd al-Raḥmān Ismā'īl b. Aḥmad al-Ḥīrī al-Nīsābūrī al-Ḍarīr (d. 430/1038).

Ff. 156. Scholar's naskh. 10 Shauwāl 752/30 Nov. 1351. No other copy appears to be recorded; for the author *see* Brockelmann, Suppl. I, 729.

149 (a) **Or. 1283 (10)**

Tuḥfat al-mulūk fī ta'bīr al-ru'yā, by Abu 'l-'Abbās Aḥmad b. Khalaf b. Aḥmad al-Sijistānī.

Ff. 87. Excellent naskh. 24 Ṣafar 763/23 Dec. 1361. Illuminated title-page and library-notice. No other copy appears to be recorded.

150 (p) **Or. 1284 (7)**

Ilāhī-nāma, by Farīd al-Dīn Muḥammad b. Ibrāhīm al-Nīshāpūrī al-'Aṭṭār (d. *ca.* 620/1223).

Ff. 126. Clear ta'līq. 10/16th century. Edited by H. Ritter (Istanbul, 1943). Ivanow 477 (3).

151 (p) **Or. 1285 (9)**

A history of Muḥammad and Early Islam down to the Battle of Kerbala, beginning missing.

Ff. 233. Clear old Persian naskh. 10 Shauwāl 729/7 Aug. 1329.

152 (a) **Or. 1287 (13)**

Qur'ān fragments (palimpsest). [Protoevangelium Jacobi et Transitus Mariae.] *See* A. Mingana and A. S. Lewis, *Leaves from three Ancient Qurâns* (Cambridge, 1914).

Ff. 94. Ancient Kufic. Undated, 1/7th century (?) Bequeathed by Mrs Agnes Smith Lewis.

153 (a) **Or. 1321–2 (9)**

Supplement to Arabic Dictionaries, by A. A. Bevan.

Ff. 570+36. European hand. 20th century. This manuscript, left incomplete at the author's death, extends as far as the word *khur'ūba*. Presented by Edwyn R. Bevan.

154 (p) **Or. 1323 (8)**

History of the Rajahs of Coorg, by Ḥusain Khān Lōhānī (fl. 1211/1796).

Ff. 226. Excellent nasta'līq. Early 13/19th century. Storey, p. 777, no. 1081. Presented by the Rev. H. C. L. Heywood, M.A.

155 (a) **Or. 1324 (12)**

Al-Qāmūs al-muḥīṭ wa'l-qābūs al-wasīṭ, by Majd al-Dīn Abu'l-Ṭāhir Muḥammad b. Ya'qūb al-Shīrāzī al-Fīrūzābādī (d. 817/1415).

Ff. 521. Excellent vocalized naskh. 11/17th century. Frequently printed. Brockelmann II, 183; Suppl. II, 234. Presented by Brigadier-General H. A. Walker, C.B., C.M.G.

156 (a) **Or. 1325 (7)**

Various extracts from the Old and New Testaments in Arabic.

Ff. 34. Clear naskh. 18th century. Some illumination. Bequeathed by W. Robertson Smith, formerly Librarian.

157 (p) **Or. 1326 (8)**

1. Account of Hamadan. Ff. 1–12.
2. Treatise on Muḥammadan Law. Ff. 13–36.
3. Account of the Tribes of Luristan. Ff. 37–57.

Ff. 57. Nasta'līq and shikasta. 14/20th century. Ex-libris E. G. Browne.

158 (p) **Or. 1328 (12)**

Tadhkirat al-shu'arā', by Daulatshāh b. 'Alā' al-Daula Bakhtīshāh al-Ghāzī al-Samarqandī (fl. 892/1487).

Ff. 432. European hand. Late 19th–early 20th century. The working-copy of E. G. Browne's edition (London, 1901).

159 (p) **Or. 1329 (12)**

Nuqṭat al-Kāf, by Mīrzā Jānī Kāshānī (d. 1852).

Ff. 296. European hand. Early 20th century. The working-copy of E. G. Browne's edition (London, 1910).

160 (a, p) **Or. 1330 (11)**

Note-book of E. G. Browne.

Ff. 74. European hand. Late 19th century. Includes rough notes made while cataloguing the Muḥammadan MSS. in the Cambridge Univ. Library.

161 (p) **Or. 1331–7 (11)**

Collation of Persian Bayán [of Mīrzā 'Alī Muḥammad the Bāb], by E. G. Browne.

Ff. 92+92+92+90+610+89+67. European hand. Late 19th century.

162 (p) **Or. 1338 (10)**

Majma' al-ansāb, by Muḥammad b. 'Alī b. Muḥammad Shabānkāra'ī (fl. 743/1343).

Ff. 98. Clear nasta'līq. 18 Rabī' I 1046/20 Aug. 1636. Storey, p. 85, no. 112.

163 (p) **Or. 1339 (10)**

Nafaḥāt al-uns, by Jāmī. *See* no. 94.

Ff. 212. Clear naskh. 2 Jumādā II 894/3 May 1489. Red margins.

164 (p) **Or. 1340 (8)**

Nusakh-i jahān-ārā, by Aḥmad b. Muḥammad Ghaffārī (d. 975/1567).

Ff. 225. Clear nasta'līq. 24 Muḥarram 1055/12 March 1645. Partly printed (ed. and tr. W. Ouseley), London, 1799. Storey, p. 116, no. 132 (2).

165 (p) **Or. 1345 (7)**

Ḥadā'iq al-siḥr fī daqā'iq al-shi'r, by Muḥammad b. 'Abd al-Jalīl 'Umarī called Rashīd-i Waṭwāṭ (d. 578/1182).

Ff. 95. Clear nasta'līq. 13/19th century. Lithographed at Teheran, 1302/1884. Rieu Suppl. no. 188.

166 (p) **Or. 1346 (7)**

Maqāmāt-i Ḥamīdī, by Ḥamīd al-Dīn 'Umar b. Maḥmūd Balkhī (d. 559/1163).

Ff. 160. Clear naskh. 13/19th century. Lithographed at Cawnpore, 1268/1851. Rieu, p. 747.

167 (p) **Or. 1347 (9)**

Dīwān, by Ẓahīr al-Dīn Abu 'l-Faḍl Ṭāhir b. Muḥammad Fāryābī (d. 598/1201).

Ff. 123. Excellent nasta'līq. 10/16th century. Lithographed several times. Ivanow 463.

168 (p) **Or. 1348 (10)**

1. *Tuḥfat al-'Irāqain*, by Afḍal al-Dīn Badīl Ibrāhīm b. 'Alī Najjār Khāqānī (d. between 582–95/1186–99). Ff. 1–59. Lithographed several times. Ivanow 461.

2. *Dīwān*, by Rahī (?). Ff. 60–118.

3. *Dīwān*, by Nūr al-Dīn Muḥammad Turshīzī Ẓuhūrī (d. *ca.* 1026/1617). Ff. 119–197. Ivanow 716.

Ff. 197. Nasta'līq. 5 Rabī' I 1023/15 April 1614.

169 (p) **Or. 1349 (10)**

1. *Tuḥfat al-'Irāqain*, by Khāqānī. Ff. 1–58.

2. *Qaṣā'id*, by Khāqānī. Ff. 59–248. Lithographed several times. Ivanow 461, 456.

Ff. 248. Clear nasta'līq. 11/17th century.

170 (p) **Or. 1350 (10)**

Kullīyāt, by Khāqāni.

Ff. 315. Good nasta'līq. 30 Jumādā I 1035/27 Feb. 1626. Lithographed several times. Ivanow 456.

171 (p) **Or. 1354 (15)**

Shāh-nāmah, by Abu 'l-Qāsim Ḥasan Firdausī (d. between 411/1020 and 421/1030).

Ff. 578. Nīm-shikastah. Date effaced, 12/18th century. Many times printed and lithographed. Ivanow 421. Presented by Major R. G. and Col. T. G. Gayer-Anderson.

172 (a, p) **Or. 1355 (13)**

1. *Qaṣīdah-i Suryānī*, with Persian interlinear translation.
2. *Du'ā-yi Kīmiyā-yi sa'ādat* (prayers in Arabic).
3. *Durūd-i Akbar* (prayers in Arabic), etc.

Ff. 44. Excellent vocalized naskh. 1000/1591–2. Illuminated 'unwāns, margins in gilt and blue. Presented by Major and Col. Gayer-Anderson.

173 (p) **Or. 1356 (10)**

Shāh-nāmah, by Firdausī.

Ff. 281. Nasta'līq. Dhu 'l-Ḥijja 972/July 1565. Illuminated 'unwāns. Twelve miniatures in Moghul style. Limp brown leather binding, signed Bahā' al-Dīn Pashāwarī, with Ḥāfiẓ Ode I tooled in relief. Presented by Major and Col. Gayer-Anderson.

174 (p) **Or. 1357 (9)**

Tārīkh-i Nādirī, by Muḥammad Mahdī b. Muḥammad Nāṣir Astarābādi (fl. 1170/1756).

Ff. 256. Clear nasta'līq. 1 Rabī' II 1199/11 Feb. 1785. Rather crude 'unwān. Many times lithographed. Storey, pp. 322–3, no. 407 (1). Presented by Major and Col. Gayer-Anderson.

175 (a) **Or. 1359 (8)**

Lisān al-falak, by Aḥmad b. 'Īsā al-Rimmiyawī al-Maghribī (fl. 960/1553).

Ff. 72. Clear scholar's naskh. 11/17th century. Brockelmann, Suppl. I, 909. Presented by Major and Col. Gayer-Anderson.

176 (p) **Or. 1362 (8)**

Subḥat al-abrār, by Jāmī. *See* no. 33.

Ff. 123. Excellent nasta'līq. 10/16th century. Illuminated 'unwān, somewhat damaged; margins in colours: floral title-bands and vignettes. Presented by Major and Col. Gayer-Anderson.

177 (a) **Or. 1367 (13)**

Various papyri fragments.

178 (p) **Or. 1368 (12)**

Muntakhab al-lubāb, by Muḥammad Hāshim Khāfī, called Khāfī Khān (d. *ca.* 1144/1731–2).

Ff. 612. Clear nasta'līq. 26 Sha'bān 1256/23 Oct. 1840. Fifteen crude miniatures. Printed at Calcutta, 1860–74, 1909–25. Storey, pp. 468–70, no. 627.

179 (a) **Or. 1369 (8)**

Al-Durr al-farīd 'ala 'l-raṣd al-jadīd, by Riḍwān Efendī al-Falaki al-Razzāz (d. 1122/1710).

Ff. 227. Excellent naskh. 6 Rabī' II 1130/9 March 1718. Illuminated 'unwān, red and blue borders, script in black, red and blue. Six illustrations. Brockelmann II, 359. Presented by Major and Col. Gayer-Anderson.

180 (a) **Or. 1370 (9)**

Qur'ān.

Ff. 273. West African hand. 24 Ramaḍān 1272/29 May 1856. Presented by Major and Col. Gayer-Anderson.

181 (p) **Or. 1385 (7)**

Dīwān, by Najm al-Dīn Ḥasan Sanjarī Dihlawī (d. 727/1327).

Ff. 158. Excellent nasta'līq. 886/1481–2. Good 'unwān in gold and blue; gold headings and gold and blue margins. Ivanow 572.

182 (p) **Or. 1386 (8)**

1. *Akhlāq-i Manṣūrī*, by Ghiyāth al-Dīn Manṣūr b. Ṣadr al-Din Muḥammad Shīrāzī (d. 948/1541). Ff. 1–95. Rieu, Suppl. 150.

2. *Auṣāf al-ashrāf*, by Naṣīr al-Dīn Muḥammad b. Muḥammad Ṭūsī (d. 672/1274). Ff. 96–134. Lithographed several times in Persia. Ivanow 1182.

Ff. 134. Excellent nasta'līq. (1) Dated 1067/1656–7; (2) 11/17th century. Margins ruled in gold and colour.

183 (p) **Or. 1388 (8)**

Dīwān, by Athīr al-Dīn Akhsikatī (d. 608/1211).

Ff. 70. Good nasta'līq. 11/17th century. Ethé, I.O. 1029.

184 (p) **Or. 1390 (10)**

Tuḥfa-yi Sāmī, by Sām Mīrzā b. Shāh Ismā'īl (d. 984/1576).

Ff. 73. Excellent nasta'līq. 1026/1617. Some illumination on ff. 1*b*–2*a*; margins ruled in gold and colours. Printed at Patna, 1934; for other copies *see* this edition.

185 (p) **Or. 1391 (10)**

A short history of the Mahrattas.

Ff. 22. Clear nasta'līq. 13/19th century. Storey, p. 764, no. 1062 (2).

186 (p) **Or. 1392 (10)**

Tuḥfa-yi tāza, by Khair al-Dīn Muḥammad Ilāhābādī (d. *c.* 1827).

Ff. 132. Clear nasta'līq. 1238/1821. English translation published Allahabad 1875. Storey, p. 702, no. 923.

187 (p) **Or. 1393 (10)**

Dīwān, by Muḥammad Taqī al-Dīn Ḥairatī (d. 961/1554).

Ff. 382. Excellent nasṭa'līq. 11/17th century. Damaged 'unwān; margins ruled in gold and colours. Ethé I.O. 1435.

188 (p) **Or. 1394 (11)**

Muḥammad-nāma, by Muḥammad Ẓuhūr b. Maulawī Ẓuhūrī (fl. 1050/1640).

Ff. 93. Nīm-shikasta. Dhu 'l-Qa'da 1183/Feb.–March 1770. Margins ruled in red and black. No other copy appears to be recorded.

189 (a) **Or. 1395** (9)

Badā'i' al-zuhūr fī waqā'i' al-duhūr (vol. II), by Zain (Shihāb) al-Dīn Abu 'l-Barakāt Muḥammad b. Aḥmad Ibn Iyās al-Nāṣirī al-Ḥanbalī (d. *ca* 930/1524).

Ff. 331. Clear naskh. 24. Ṣafar 919/1 May 1513. Printed at Bulaq, 1311–12/1893–94; Leipzig, 1931–6. Brockelmann II, 295; Suppl. II, 405–6.

190 (a) **Or. 1396** (9)

1. *Wafayāt qaum min al-Miṣrīyīn*, by Abū Isḥāq Ibrāhīm b. Sa'īd b. 'Abd Allāh al-Nu'mānī al-Ḥabbāl (d. 482/1089). Ff. 1–20. Brockelmann, Suppl. I, 572.

2. *Ta'rīkh 'ulamā' ahl Miṣr*, by Abu'l-Qāsim Yaḥyā b. 'Alī al-Ḥaḍramī Ibn al-Ṭaḥḥān (d. 416/1025). Ff. 21-58. Brockelmann, Suppl. I, 571.

3. *Hawātif al-jinān*, by Abū Bakr Muḥammad b. Ja'far al-Kharā'iṭī (d. 327/938). Ff. 59–83. Brockelmann, Suppl. I, 250.

Ff. 83. Clear naskh. Early 14/20th century.

191 (p) **Or. 1397** (10)

Fawā'id-i Ṣafawīya, by Abu 'l-Ḥasan b. Ibrāhīm Qazwīnī (fl. 1210/1795).

Ff. 876. Clear nasta'līq. Early 13/19th century. Fine illuminated 'unwān, margins ruled in gold and colours. Storey, p. 320, no. 402.

192 (p) **Or. 1398** (11)

Haft iqlīm, by Amīn Aḥmad Rāzī (fl. 1002/1594).

Ff. 479. Nasta'līq. 11 Rabī' II 1089/2 June 1678. Publication (*Bibliotheca Indica*) begun in 1918. Ivanow 282.

193 (p) **Or. 1399** (11)

Aḥwāl-i firqa-yi Sikhān, by Khwush-waqt Rāy (fl. 1811).

Ff. 74. Clear nasta'līq. 13/19th century. Storey p. 668, no. 847.

194 (p) **Or. 1400** (11)

Bēg-Lār-nāma, by Idrākī Bēg-Lārī Tattawī (fl. 1010/1601).

Ff. 437. Excellent nasta'līq. 9 Jumādā I 1233/17 March 1818. Fine illuminated 'unwān; margins ruled in gold. Storey, p. 654, no. 825.

195 (p) **Or. 1401 (11)**

Mujmal al-ta'rīkh-i ba'd-Nādirīya, by Abu 'l-Ḥasan b. Muḥammad Amīn (fl. 1164/1750).

Ff. 147. Clear nasta'līq. 6 Dhu 'l-Ḥijja 1245/29 May 1830. Partly printed at Leiden, 1891. Storey p. 330, no. 415.

196 (a) **Or. 1402 (11)**

'Iqd al-jawāhir wa'l-durar, by Jamāl al-Dīn Abū 'Alawī Muḥammad b. Abī Bakr b. Aḥmad al-Shillī al-Ḥaḍramī (d. 1093/1682).

Ff. 199. Clear naskh. 1329/1911. Brockelmann II, 383; Suppl. II, 516.

197 (a) **Or. 1403 (10)**

Dhail Ta'rīkh Baghdād (vol. x), by Muḥibb al-Dīn Abū 'Abd Allāh Muḥammad b. Maḥmūd b. al-Najjār al-Baghdādī (d. 643/1245).

Ff. 709. Clear naskh. 17 Sha'bān 1330/1 Aug. 1912. Brockelmann, Suppl. I, 563.

198 (a) **Or. 1404 (11)**

Al-Sanā' al-bāhir bi-takmīl al-Nūr al-sāfir, by Abū 'Alawī al-Shillī.

Ff. 253. Clear naskh. 1326/1908. Brockelmann II, 383, Suppl. II, 516.

199 (a) **Or. 1405 (10)**

1. *Kitāb fi'l-rumḥ wa-ghairih*, by Saif al-Dīn Tuquz. Ff. 1–53. [? = *Bunūd al-rumḥ, see* Brockelmann, Suppl. II, 167.]

2. *Al-Nafaḥāt al-'anbarīya*, by Shihāb al-Dīn Abu'l-'Abbās Aḥmad b. Muḥammad al-Maqqarī al-Tilimsānī (d. 1041/1632). Ff. 54–149. Brockelmann II, 297; Suppl. II, 408.

3. Hand-list of certain MSS. in the Damascus Public Library. Ff. 150–205.

Ff. 205. Clear naskh. 1328–33/1910–15.

200 (p) **Or. 1406 (10)**

1. *Tārīkh-i Maḥmūd*, by Maḥmud b. Khwānd-Amīr (fl. 950/1543). Ff. 1–103. 16 Muḥarram 1047/10 June 1637. Storey, p. 304, no. 378.

2. *Rauḍat al-ṣafā' (khātima)*, by Muḥammad b. Khāwand-Shāh b. Maḥmūd called Mīr Khwānd (d. 903/1498). Ff. 104–176. 12 Rajab 1047/30 Nov. 1637. Lithographed several times in India and Persia. Storey, p. 93, no. 123.

Ff. 176. Good nasta'līq.

201 (p) **Or. 1407 (11)**

Majma' al-tawārīkh, by Pandit Bīrbal, called Kāchar (fl. 1250/1834).

Ff. 225. Clear nasta'līq. 13/19th century. Storey, p. 685, no. 883.

202 (p) **Or. 1408 (13)**

Shāh-'Ālam-nāma, by Munshī Munnā Lāl (fl. 1220/1805).

Ff. 217. Clear nasta'līq. Early 13/19th century. Storey, p. 644, no. 809.

203 (p) **Or. 1409 (14)**

Tārīkh-i Baihaqī, by Abu'l-Faḍl Muḥammad b. al-Ḥusain al-Baihaqī (d. 470/1077).

Ff. 197. Clear nasta'līq. 7 Rabī' I 1281/10 Aug. 1864. Printed at Calcutta, 1861–2, Teheran, 1307/1890. Storey, p. 253, no. 334.

204 (a) **Or. 1410 (13)**

Nasamat al-saḥar (vol. I), by Ḍiyā' al-Dīn Abū Isḥāq Yūsuf b. Yaḥyā b. al-Ḥusain al-Ḥasanī al-Ṣan'ānī (fl. 1111/1700).

Ff. 446. Clear naskh. 26 Shauwāl 1318/16 Feb. 1901. Brockelmann II, 403; Suppl. II, 552.

205 (a) **Or. 1411 (13)**

Nasamat al-saḥar (vol. II), by al-Ṣan'ānī.

Ff. 464. Clear naskh. 23 Rabī' I 1320/30 June 1902.

206 (p) **Or. 1412 (14)**

Sharaf-nāma-yi shāhī, by Ḥāfiẓ Tanīsh b. Mīr Muḥammad al-Bukhārī (fl. 996/1588).

Ff. 433. Clear nasta'līq. 12/18th century. Storey, p. 374, no. 504.

207 (a) **Or. 1415 (9)**

Ghawānī al-ashwāq fī ma'ānī al-'ushshāq by 'Abd al-Mu'īn b. Aḥmad al-Bakkā' al-Ḥanafī (fl. 10/16th century).

Ff. 71. Clear scholar's naskh. Undated. 11/17th century. Brockelmann, Suppl. II, 383, 570. R. A. Nicholson Bequest.

208 (a) **Or. 1416 (10)**

Kanz al-'irfān fī fiqh al-Qur'ān, by al-Miqyād b. 'Abd Allāh b. Muḥammad al-Suyūrī al-Asadī al-Ḥillī (fl. 800/1397).

Ff. 226. Excellent naskh. Dhu 'l-Qa'da 1065/Sept. 1655. Lithographed at Teheran, 1314/1896; Tabriz, 1314/1896. Brockelmann, Suppl. II, 209. R. A. Nicholson Bequest.

209 (a) **Or. 1417 (7)**

Zahr al-kimām fī qiṣṣat Yūsuf ('alaih al-salām), by Sirāj al-Dīn Abū Ḥafṣ 'Umar b. Ibrāhīm b. 'Umar al-Anṣārī al-Ausī al-Mursī (fl. 683/1284).

Ff. 244. Good scholar's naskh. 25 Jumādā II 846/31 Oct. 1442. Illuminated sarlauḥ. Often printed. Brockelmann II, 265; Suppl. II, 378. R. A. Nicholson Bequest.

210 (a) **Or. 1418 (13)**

al-Khawāṣṣ al-mujarraba, by Abu'l-'Alā' Zuhr b. 'Abd al-Malik b. Muḥammad b. Marwān Ibn Zuhr al-Ishbīlī (d. 525/1131).

Ff. 37. Clear naskh. Undated, 11/17th century. Brockelmann I, 486; Suppl. I, 889. R. A. Nicholson Bequest.

211 (a) **Or. 1419 (7)**

Al-Ghinā wa'l-munā, by Abū Manṣūr al-Ḥasan b. Nūḥ al-Qumrī (d. *ca.* 380/990).

Ff. 352. Clear naskh. 29 Jumādā I 924/8 June 1518. Slight 'unwān. Brockelmann I, 239; Suppl. I, 425. R. A. Nicholson Bequest.

212 (a) **Or. 1420 (8)**

Hazz al-quḥūf bi-sharḥ Qaṣīdat Abi'l-Shādūf (vol. I), by Yūsuf b. Muḥammad b. 'Abd al-Jawād al-Shirbīnī (fl. 1098/1687).

Ff. 99. Clear naskh. 30 Muḥarram 1146/13 July 1733. Printed several times at Cairo. Brockelmann II, 278; Suppl. II, 387. R. A. Nicholson Bequest.

213 (a) **Or. 1421 (8)**

Hazz al-quḥūf (vol. II), by al-Shirbīnī.

Ff. 124. Clear naskh. 26 Ṣafar 1146/8 Aug. 1733. R. A. Nicholson Bequest.

214 (a) **Or. 1422 (8)**

Al-Fatḥ al-alī fī sharḥ baitai 'l-Mauṣilī, by Aḥmad b. 'Abd al-Laṭīf al-Barbīr al-Ḥasanī al-Bairūtī (d. 1226/1811).

Ff. 213. Clear naskh. Dhu 'l-Qa'da 1248/March-April 1833. Illuminated 'unwān. Printed at Beirut, 1302/1885. Brockelmann, Suppl. II, 750. R. A. Nicholson Bequest.

215 (a) **Or. 1423 (7)**

Aṭbāq al-dhahab, by Shufurwa (fl. 600/1203). *See* no. 46(2).

Ff. 65. Clear scholar's naskh. 3 Sha'bān 808/24 Jan. 1406. R. A. Nicholson Bequest.

216 (a) **Or. 1424 (8)**

Sharḥ al-Bahjat al-marḍīya, by Muḥammad Ṣāliḥ b. Ibrāhīm b. Ḥusain al-Aḥsā'ī al-Ḥakīm (fl. 1073/1662).

Ff. 224. Two clear naskh hands. Undated 12/18th century. Brockelmann I, 299; Suppl. I, 525. R. A. Nicholson Bequest.

217 (a) **Or. 1425 (12)**

Al-Jawāhir al-zakīya fī 'ilm al-daurat al-zamānīya, by 'Alī b. 'Abd al-Ṣādiq al-'Abbādī al-Ṭarābulusī al-Jabālī.

Ff. 184. Clear maghribī. Undated, 12/18th century. No other copy appears to be recorded. R. A. Nicholson Bequest.

218 (a) **Or. 1426 (8)**

Nūr al-'ain sharḥ Silk al-'ain, by 'Alī b. 'Aṭīya b. Ḥasan al-Ḥaddād 'Alawān al-Ḥamawī (d. 936/1530).

Ff. 209. Clear naskh. 14 Sha'bān 1062/21 July 1652. Brockelmann II, 123; Suppl. II, 153. R. A. Nicholson Bequest.

219 (a) **Or. 1427 (10)**

Sulāfat al-'aṣr fī maḥāsin a'yān al-'aṣr, by Ṣadr al-Dīn 'Alī Khān b. Aḥmad b. Muḥammad Ma'ṣūm al-Ḥusainī al-Ḥasanī al-Madanī (d. 1117/1705 or 1120/1708).

Ff. 328. Excellent naskh. 5 Jumādā II, 1082/9 Oct. 1671. Illuminated 'unwāns on ff. 5*b*–6*a*, margins ruled throughout in gold, black and red. Printed at Cairo, 1324/1906, 1334/1916. Brockelmann II, 421; Suppl. II, 627–8. R. A. Nicholson Bequest.

220 (a) **Or. 1428** (10)

1. *Irshād al-qāṣid ilā asnā al-maqāṣid*, by Ibn al-Akfānī (d. 749/1348). Ff. 1–66. *See* no. 126.

2. *Ghunyat al-labīb fīmā yusta'mal 'inda ghaibat al-ṭabīb*, by the same author. Ff. 67–92. Brockelmann II, 136.

3. *Nukhab al-dhakhā'ir fī aḥwāl al-jawāhir*, by the same author. Ff. 93–104. Printed at Beirut, 1908. Brockelmann II, 136; Suppl. II, 169.

Ff. 104. 20 Jumādā I 749/16 Aug. 1348. R. A. Nicholson Bequest.

221 (a) **Or. 1429** (7)

Three tales from *Alf laila wa-laila* ('The Arabian Nights').

Ff. 153. Clear naskh. Undated, 11/17th century. Printed often. Brockelmann II, 58–62; Suppl. II, 59–63. R. A. Nicholson Bequest.

222 (a) **Or. 1430** (8)

Sharḥ al-Muqaddimat al-Ājurrūmīya, by Zain al-Dīn Khālid b. 'Abd Allāh b. Abī Bakr al-Azharī al-Waqqād (d. 905/1499).

Ff. 20. Clear naskh. Undated, 11/17th century. Often printed at Cairo. Brockelmann II, 238; Suppl. II, 333. R. A. Nicholson Bequest.

223 (a) **Or. 1431** (8)

Bughyat al-murtād li-taṣḥīḥ al-ḍād, by Nūr al-Dīn 'Alī b. Muḥammad b. 'Alī b. Ghānim al-Maqdisī al-Ṭūrī al-Khazrajī (d. 1004/1595).

Ff. 25. Clear scholar's naskh. 3 Ramaḍān 1016/22 Dec. 1607. Brockelmann II, 312; Suppl. II, 429. R. A. Nicholson Bequest.

224 (a) **Or. 1432** (12)

Al-Kashkūl, by Bahā' al-Dīn Muḥammad b. Ḥusain b. 'Abd al-Ṣamad al-Ḥārithī al-Jubba'ī al-'Āmilī al-Bahā'ī (d. 1030/1621).

Ff. 331. Clear ta'līq and naskh. 1056/1646. Illuminated 'unwāns on ff. 2*b*, 66*b*, 109*b*, 191*b*, 262*b*. Printed in Persia, India and Egypt. Brockelmann II, 415; Suppl. II, 596. R. A. Nicholson Bequest.

225 (a) **Or. 1433 (9)**

Miftāḥ al-jafr al-jāmi'; and other magical tracts, by 'Abd al-Raḥmān b. Muḥammad b. 'Alī al-Bisṭāmī al-Ḥanafī al-Ḥurūfī (d. 858/1454).

Ff. 109. Naskh. Undated. 11/17th century. Diagrams and crude drawings. Brockelmann, II, 232; Suppl. II, 324. R. A. Nicholson Bequest.

226 (a) **Or. 1434 (8)**

Al-Ta'arruf li-madhhab ahl al-taṣauwuf, by Abū Bakr Muḥammad b. Isḥāq b. Ibrāhīm al-Kalābādhī al-Bukhārī (d. between 380/990 and 390/1000).

Ff. 33. Clear scholar's naskh, mid-Rabī' II 700/Dec. 1300. Printed at Cairo, 1933. Brockelmann I, 200; Suppl. I, 360. R. A. Nicholson Bequest.

227 (a) **Or. 1435 (11)**

Ḥayāt al-ḥayawān, by Kamāl al-Dīn Muḥammad b. Mūsā al-Damīrī (d. 808/1405).

Ff. 144. Small, clear scholar's naskh. 5 Ṣafar 879/21 June 1474. Printed often in Egypt. Brockelmann II, 138; Suppl. II, 171. R. A. Nicholson Bequest.

228 (a) **Or. 1436 (10)**

Ḥayāt al-ḥayawān. Another copy.

Ff. 424. Clear naskh. Undated, 11/17 century. R. A. Nicholson Bequest.

229 (a) **Or. 1437 (10)**

Ḥayāt al-ḥayawān. Another copy.

Ff. 149. Excellent nasta'līq. Ramaḍān 1021/Oct.–Nov. 1612. R. A. Nicholson Bequest.

230 (a) **Or. 1438 (7)**

Dhail Ta'rīkh al-Islām (*lil-Dhahabī*), by Shams al-Dīn Abu 'l-Maḥāsin Muḥammad b. 'Alī b. Ḥamza al-Ḥusainī al-Dimashqī (d. 763/1362).

Ff. 37. Cursive naskh. Undated, 8/14th century. Brockelmann II, 47; Suppl. II, 46. R. A. Nicholson Bequest.

231 (a) **Or. 1439 (12)**

Akhbār al-duwal wa-āthār al-uwal, by Abu 'l-'Abbās Aḥmad b. Yūsuf al-Dimashqī al-Qaramānī (d. 1019/1611).

Ff. 200. Clear scholar's naskh. Dhu 'l-Ḥijja 1138/Aug. 1726. Lithographed at Baghdād, 1283/1866, printed at Cairo, 1290/1873. Brockelmann II, 301; Suppl. II, 412. R. A. Nicholson Bequest.

232 (a) **Or. 1440 (9)**

Ṭahārat al-qulūb wa'l-khuḍū' li-'Allām al-ghuyūb, by 'Izz al-Dīn Abū Muḥammad 'Abd al-'Azīz b. Aḥmad b. Sa'īd al-Dīrīnī al-Damīrī al-Dahrī (d. 697/1297).

Ff. 100. Clear naskh. End of Jumādā II 1158/July 1745. Printed at Cairo 1296/1879, 1305/1888, 1329/1911. Brockelmann I, 452; Suppl. I, 811. R. A. Nicholson Bequest.

233 (a) **Or. 1441–2 (12)**

Ta'rīkh al-khamīs fī aḥwāl anfas al-nafīs, by Ḥusain b. Muḥammad b. al-Ḥasan al-Diyārbakrī (d. 970/1582).

Ff. 385 and 401. Clear naskh. Undated, 11/17th century. Margins ruled in red. Brockelmann II, 381; Suppl. II, 514. R. A. Nicholson Bequest.

234 (a) **Or. 1443 (8)**

Al-Durrat al-munīfa 'alā madhhab al-Imām al-a'ẓam Abī Ḥanīfa, by 'Umar b. 'Umar al-Dafrī al-Zuhrī al-Azharī al-Ḥanafī (d. 1079/1668).

Ff. 67. Excellent naskh. 26 Rajab 1077/22 January 1667. Brockelmann II, 314; Suppl. II, 432. R. A. Nicholson Bequest.

235 (a) **Or. 1444 (8)**

Ḥāshiya 'ala 'l-Muṭauwal, by Ḥasan Chelebī b. Muḥammad Shāh b. al-Fanārī (d. 886/1481).

Ff. 524. Clear naskh. 20 Jumādā I 1025/5 June 1616. Printed at Istanbul, 1854. Brockelmann, I, 295; Suppl. I, 517. R. A. Nicholson Bequest.

236 (a) **Or. 1445 (8)**

Sharḥ 'Uyūn al-ḥikma (pts. 2–3), by Fakhr al-Dīn Abū

'Abd Allāh 'Umar b. al-Ḥusain b. al-Khaṭīb al-Rāzī (d. 606/1209).

Ff. 254. Good naskh. Undated, 12/18th century. Brockelmann I, 455; Suppl. I, 817. R. A. Nicholson Bequest.

237 (a) **Or. 1446** (9)

1. *Al-Jāsūs 'ala 'l-Qāmūs*, by Aḥmad Fāris b. Yūsuf b. Manṣūr al-Shidyāq (d. 1305/1887). Ff. 1–80. Printed at Istanbul, 1299/1882. Brockelmann II, 183.

2. *Sirr al-layāl fi 'l-qalb wa'l-ibdāl*, by the same author. Ff. 81–140. Printed at Istanbul, 1284/1857. Brockelmann II, 506.

Ff. 141. Excellent naskh. Holograph, dated 27 Ramaḍān 1266/7 August 1850. R. A. Nicholson Bequest.

238 (a) **Or. 1447** (10)

Al-Qāmūs al-muḥīt, by al-Fīrūzābādī. *See* no. 155.

Ff. 642. Fine small naskh. Undated, 11/17th century. Fine decorated 'unwān, margins in gold and colours throughout. R. A. Nicholson Bequest.

239 (a) **Or. 1448** (9)

Al-Tadhkira, by Jabrā'īl b. Farḥāt (d. 1732).

Ff. 176. Excellent naskh. Undated, 12/18th century. Printed thrice at Beirut. Brockelmann, Suppl. II, 389. R. A. Nicholson Bequest.

240 (a) **Or. 1449** (9)

Baḥth al-maṭālib wa-khaṭṭ al-ṭālib, by Jabrā'īl b. Farḥāt.

Ff. 133. Excellent naskh. Undated, late 12/18th century. Printed at Malta, 1836, and thrice at Beirut. Brockelmann, Suppl. II, 389. R. A. Nicholson Bequest.

241 (a) **Or. 1450** (8)

1. *'Ilāj al-masākīn wa-ṭibb al-fuqarā'* ascribed to Galen. Ff. 2–53.

2. *Faṣl fi 'l-iktiḥāl*. Ff. 54–63.

3. Medical prescriptions. Ff. 64–124.

4. Medical prescriptions. Ff. 125–219.

Ff. 213. Clear naskh. 29 Jumādā I 1151/15 Sept. 1738. R. A. Nicholson Bequest.

242 (a) **Or. 1451 (8)**

Al-Sīrat al-Ḥalabīya (vol. III), by Nūr al-Dīn Abu 'l-Faraj 'Alī b. Ibrāhīm b. Aḥmad al-Ḥalabī al-Qāhirī al-Shāfi'ī al-Aḥmadī (d. 1044/1635).

Ff. 376. Clear naskh. 11 Ṣafar 1150/10 June 1737. Printed several times at Cairo. Brockelmann II, 307; Suppl. II, 418. R. A. Nicholson Bequest.

243 (a) **Or. 1452 (7)**

1. *Rasā'il* (here called *Mukātabāt*), by Badī' al-Zamān Abu 'l-Faḍl Aḥmad b. al-Ḥusain b. Yaḥyā al-Hamadhānī (d. 398/1007). Ff. 1–68. Printed at Beirut and Cairo. Brockelmann, Suppl I, 152.

2. *Maqāmāt*, by the same author. Ff. 69–122. Frequently printed. Brockelmann I, 95, Suppl. I, 152.

Ff. 122. Clear naskh. 1814. R. A. Nicholson Bequest.

244 (a) **Or. 1453 (10)**

Al-Maqāmāt (section), by Badī' al-Zamān al-Hamadhānī.

Ff. 31. Clear naskh. Undated, 13/19th century. R. A. Nicholson Bequest.

245 (a) **Or. 1454 (8)**

Nuzhat al-akhyār wa-majma' al-nawādir wa'l-akhbār, by Muḥammad b. Abi 'l-Wafā' b. Ma'rūf al-Khalwatī al-Ḥamawī (fl. 1032/1622).

Ff. 123. Clear naskh. Undated, 11/17th century. Brockelmann II, 302. R. A. Nicholson Bequest.

246 (a) **Or. 1455 (9)**

Al-Waḍ'īya fī ma'ālim al-dīn, by Ḥamīd al-Dīn Aḥmad b. 'Abd Allāh al-Kirmānī (d. *ca.* 408/1017).

Ff. 106. Clear modern naskh. 8 Dhu 'l-Ḥijja 1347/18 May 1929. Ivanow Guide no. 124. R. A. Nicholson Bequest.

247 (a) **Or. 1456 (9)**

Sharḥ Hidāyat al-ḥikma, by Maulānā-zāda Aḥmad b. Maḥmūd al-Harawī.

Ff. 112. Scholar's ta'līq. Undated, 10/16th century. Brockelmann I, 464; Suppl. I, 840. R. A. Nicholson Bequest.

248 (a) **Or. 1457** (8)

Ḥāshiya 'ala 'l-Mukhtaṣar, by Quṭb al-Dīn Aḥmad b. Muḥammad b. Yaḥyā b. Sa'd al-Dīn al-Taftazānī al-Ḥafīd (d. 906/1500).

Ff. 69. Clear ta'līq. Undated, 11/17th century. Illuminated 'unwān, gilt and black margins. Printed at Calcutta 1280/1863. Brockelmann I, 295; Suppl. I, 518. R. A. Nicholson Bequest.

249 (a) **Or. 1458** (8)

Durrat al-ghauwāṣ fī auhām al-khauwāṣ, by Abū Muḥammad al-Qāsim b. 'Alī b. Muḥammad al-Ḥarīrī (d. 516/1122).

Ff. 68. Good ta'līq. Undated, 10/16th century. Printed several times at Cairo. Brockelmann I, 277; Suppl. I, 488. R. A. Nicholson Bequest.

250 (a) **Or. 1459** (7)

Dīwān al-ṣabāba, by Shihāb al-Dīn Abu 'l-'Abbās Aḥmad b. Yaḥyā Ibn Abī Ḥajala al-Tilimsānī al-Ḥanbalī (d. 776/1375).

Ff. 88. Scholar's naskh. 5 Muḥarram 840/20 July 1436. Printed several times at Cairo. Brockelmann II, 13; Suppl. II, 5–6. R. A. Nicholson Bequest.

251 (a) **Or. 1460** (8)

Sukkardān al-sulṭān, by Ibn Abī Ḥajala.

Ff. 77. Good scholar's naskh. Undated, 12/18th century. Printed several times at Cairo. Brockelmann II, 13; Suppl. II, 6. R. A. Nicholson Bequest.

252 (a) **Or. 1461** (10)

'Uyūn al-anbā', by Muwaffaq al-Dīn Abu'l-'Abbās Aḥmad b. al-Qāsim b. Abī Uṣaibi'a al-Sa'dī al-Khazrajī (d. 668/1270).

Ff. 336. Clear ta'līq. 5 Dhu 'l-Ḥijja 1136/25 Aug. 1724. Margins ruled in red. Printed at Königsberg (Cairo), 1884. Brockelmann I, 325; Suppl. I, 560. R. A. Nicholson Bequest.

253 (a) **Or. 1462** (9)

Fatḥ al-dhakhā'ir wa'l-aghlāq 'an wajh Tarjumān al-ashwāq (here called *al-Dhakhā'ir wa'l-aghlāq fī sharḥ Tarjumān al-ashwāq*), by Muḥyī al-Dīn Abū 'Abd Allāh Muḥammad b. 'Alī b. Muḥammad Ibn 'Arabī al-Ḥātimī al-Ṭā'ī (d. 638/1240).

Ff. 140. Clear naskh. 21 Ṣafar 1029/27 January 1620. Printed thrice at Beirut. Brockelmann I, 447; Suppl. I, 799–800. R. A. Nicholson Bequest.

254 (a) **Or. 1463 (9)**

1. *Asmā' al-rijāl*, by Shams al-Dīn Muḥammad b. 'Abd Allāh al-Khaṭīb al-Tibrīzī al-'Umarī (fl. 740/1339). Ff. 1–72. Printed twice in India. Brockelmann I, 364; Suppl II, 262.

2. *Nuzhat al-qulūb fī tafsīr gharīb al-Qur'ān*, by Abū Bakr Muḥammad b. 'Umar b. Aḥmad b. 'Uzair al-'Uzairī al-Sijistānī (d. 330/941). Ff. 73–136. Printed at Cairo, 1295/1878. Brockelmann I, 119; Suppl. I, 183.

Ff. 137. Clear naskh. 20 Muḥarram 916/29 April 1510. R. A. Nicholson Bequest.

255 (a) **Or. 1464 (8)**

1. *Dīwān*, by Ḥasan Bey al-A'ūjī (fl. 11/17th century). Ff. 1–55. No other copy appears to be recorded.

2. *Dīwān*, by Ḥusain b. Aḥmad b. Ḥusain al-Jazarī al-Ḥalabī (d. 1034/1625). Ff. 56–118. Printed at Aleppo, 1347/1929. Brockelmann II, 274; Suppl. II, 385.

Ff. 118. Excellent naskh. Rajab 1034/April 1625. R. A. Nicholson Bequest.

256 (a) **Or. 1465 (10)**

Badā'i' al-zuhūr fī waqā'i' al-duhūr (vol. I), by Ibn Iyās. *See* no. 189.

Ff. 256. Clear naskh. Undated 11/17th century. R. A. Nicholson Bequest.

257 (a) **Or. 1466 (8)**

Sharḥ al-Qaṣīdat al-'Abdūnīya, by 'Abd al-Malik b. 'Abd Allāh b. Badrūn al-Ḥaḍramī al-Shilbī (fl. 560/1164).

Ff. 149. Clear naskh. Undated, 12/18th century. Printed at Leiden, 1846; Cairo, 1340/1921. Brockelmann I, 271; Suppl. I, 480. R. A. Nicholson Bequest.

258 (a) **Or. 1467–8** (**12**)

Jāmi' mufradāt al-adwiya wa'l-aghdhiya, by Ḍiyā' al-Dīn Abū 'Abd Allāh Muḥammad b. Aḥmad al-Malaqī Ibn al-Baiṭār (d. 646/1248).

Ff. 123+239. Several clear naskh hands. Undated, 11/17th century. Printed at Bulaq, 1291/1874. Brockelmann I, 492; Suppl. I, 897. R. A. Nicholson Bequest.

259 (a) **Or. 1469–70** (**9**)

Tuḥfat al-nuẓẓār fī gharā'ib al-amṣār, by Abū 'Abd Allāh Muḥammad b. 'Abd Allāh b. Muḥammad Ibn Baṭṭūta al-Lawāṭī al-Ṭanjī (d. 779/1377).

Ff. 312+279. Rather cursive maghribī. Undated, early 13/19th century. Printed several times at Paris and Cairo. Brockelmann II, 256; Suppl. II, 366. R. A. Nicholson Bequest.

260 (a) **Or. 1471** (**9**)

Al-Shāfiya, by Jamāl al-Dīn Abū 'Amr 'Uthmān b. 'Umar b. Abī Bakr Ibn al-Ḥājib (d. 646/1249).

Ff. 145. Good naskh. 12/18th century. Printed frequently. Brockelmann I, 305; Suppl. I, 535. R. A. Nicholson Bequest.

261 (a) **Or. 1472** (**9**)

Sharḥ al-Shāfiya.

Ff. 253. Good naskh. Undated, 12/18th century. *See* Brockelmann I, 305; Suppl. I, 536–7. R. A. Nicholson Bequest.

262 (a) **Or. 1473** (**10**)

Man ṣabara ẓafara, by Abū Bakr Muḥammad b. 'Alī b. 'Umar al-Muṭṭauwi'ī al-Ghāzī al-Nīsābūrī (fl. 435/1043).

Ff. 132. Clear scholar's naskh. Undated, 9/15th century. No other copy appears to be recorded; *see* Brockelmann, Suppl. I, 601. R. A. Nicholson Bequest.

263 (a) **Or. 1474** (**9**)

Mughnī al-labīb 'an kutub al-a'ārīb, by Jamāl al-Dīn Abū Muḥammad 'Abd Allāh b. Yūsuf Ibn Hishām (d. 761/1360).

Ff. 281. Clear naskh. 15 Shauwāl 1181/5 March 1768. Frequently printed in Persia and at Cairo. Brockelmann II, 23; Suppl. II, 17. R. A. Nicholson Bequest.

264 (a) **Or. 1475 (11)**

Shadharāt al-dhahab fī akhbār man dhahab (first half), by Abu'l-Falāḥ 'Abd al-Ḥaiy b. Aḥmad b. Muḥammad Ibn al-'Imād al-'Akarī al-Ṣāliḥī al-Ḥanbalī (d. 1089/1679).

Ff. 342. Good scholar's naskh. 1087/1676–7. Printed at Cairo, 1350/1931–2. Brockelmann II, 383; Suppl. II, 403. R. A. Nicholson Bequest.

265 (a) **Or. 1476 (7)**

1. *Shudhūr al-'uqūd fī ta'rīkh al-'uhūd*, by Jamāl al-Dīn Abu 'l-Faraj 'Abd al-Raḥmān b. 'Alī Ibn al-Jauzī (d. 597/1200). Ff. 1–69. 1 Sha'bān 1003/11 April 1595. Brockelmann I, 502; Suppl. I, 915.

2. *Tuḥfat al-ẓurafā' fī ta'rīkh al-khulafā*, by Shams al-Dīn Abū 'Abd Allāh Muḥammad b. Aḥmad al-Bā'ūnī al-Shāfi'ī al-Dimashqī (d. 871/1465). Ff. 70–88. Undated, *ca.* 1003/1594–5. Brockelmann II, 41; Suppl. II, 38.

3. *Al-Qaul al-sadīd al-aẓraf fī sīrat al-Malik al-Sa'īd al-Ashraf* (with supplement), by Muḥammad b. Yūsuf b. Aḥmad al-Bā'ūnī al-Shāfi'ī (d. 910/1505). Ff. 89–111. Same hand. Brockelmann II, 54.

4. Extract from *al-Durr al-fākhir li-a'yān al-qarn al-'āshir*, by Muḥammad b. 'Abd al-'Azīz b. 'Umar b. Muḥammad Ibn Fahd al-Hāshimī al-Makkī al-Shāfi'ī al-Atharī (d. 954/1547). Ff. 112–122. Same hand. No other copy appears to be recorded.

Ff. 122. R. A. Nicholson Bequest.

266 (a) **Or. 1477 (8)**

Qalā'id al-'iqyān fī maḥāsin al-a'yān, by Abū Naṣr al-Fatḥ b. Muḥammad b. 'Ubaid Allāh Ibn Khāqān al-Qaisī (d. 529/1134 or 535/1140).

Ff. 71. Clear scholar's naskh. Undated, 9/15th century. Printed at Paris, 1277/1860; Bulaq, 1283/1866, 1284/1867. Brockelmann I, 339; Suppl. I, 579. R. A. Nicholson Bequest.

267 (a) **Or. 1478 (10)**

Sharḥ Alfīyat Ibn Mālik, by 'Abd Allāh b. 'Abd al-Raḥmān b. 'Abd Allāh Ibn 'Aqīl al-Shāfi'ī al-Qurashī (d. 769/1367).

Ff. 309. Good naskh. 11/17th century. Printed frequently at Cairo, and Leipzig, 1851. Brockelmann I, 299; Suppl. I, 523. R. A. Nicholson Bequest.

268 (a) **Or. 1479** (10)

1. *Al-Alfīya*, by Jamāl al-Dīn Muḥammad b. 'Abd Allāh Ibn Mālik al-Ṭā'ī al-Jaiyānī (d. 672/1274). Ff. 1–40.

2. *Auḍaḥ al-masālik ilā Alfīyat Ibn Mālik*, by Jamāl al-Dīn Abū Muḥammad 'Abd Allāh b. Yūsuf Ibn Hishām (d. 761/1360). Ff. 44–136.

Ff. 138. Good nasta'līq. 11 Ramaḍān 1094/3 Sept. 1683. Both works frequently printed. Brockelmann I, 298–9; Suppl. II, 522–5. R. A. Nicholson Bequest.

269 (a) **Or. 1480** (8)

Al-Ta'līq min kitāb al-'Umda fī maḥāsin al-shi'r wa-ādābih li-Abī 'Alī Ḥasan b. Rashīq.

Ff. 179. Good scholar's naskh. 10 Shauwāl 1067/22 July 1657. *See* Brockelmann, Suppl. I, 540. R. A. Nicholson Bequest.

270 (a) **Or. 1481** (9)

Rauḍat al-manāẓir fī akhbār ('ilm) al-awā'il wa'l-awākhir, by Zain (Muḥibb, Muḥyī) al-Dīn Abu 'l-Walīd Muḥammad b. Muḥammad b. Maḥmud Ibn al-Shiḥna al-Ḥalabī al-Ḥanafī (d. 815/1412).

Ff. 154. Clear naskh. Undated, 11/17th century. Printed at Bulaq, 1290/1873. Brockelmann II, 142; Suppl. II, 177. R. A. Nicholson Bequest.

271 (a) **Or. 1482** (10)

Fuṣūṣ al-ḥikam, by Muḥyī al-Dīn Abū 'Abd Allāh Muḥammad b. 'Alī b. Muḥammad Ibn 'Arabī al-Ḥātimī al-Ṭā'ī (d. 638/1240).

Ff. 151. Excellent scholar's naskh. Rabī' I 788/April 1386. Printed frequently. Brockelmann I, 442; Suppl. I, 792. R. A. Nicholson Bequest.

272 (a) **Or. 1483** (8)

Al-Fawā'id al-Ḍiyā'īya, by Jāmī (d. 898/1492).

Ff. 271. Clear ta'līq. Muḥarram 1005/Aug.–Sept. 1597. Often lithographed in India and printed in Turkey. Brockelmann I, 304; Suppl. I, 533. R. A. Nicholson Bequest.

273 (a) **Or. 1484 (7)**

Taqrīb al-nashr, by Shams al-Dīn Abu 'l-Khair Muḥammad b. Muḥammad al-Jazarī al-Qurashī al-Dimashqī al-Shīrāzī (d. 833/1429).

Ff. 86. Clear scholar's naskh. 18 Rajab 833/12 April 1430. Brockelmann II, 202; Suppl. II, 274. R. A. Nicholson Bequest.

274 (a) **Or. 1485 (9)**

1. *Kashf al-asrār 'an ḥikam al-ṭuyūr wa'l-azhār*, by 'Izz al-Dīn 'Abd al-Salām b. Aḥmad Ibn Ghānim al-Maqdisī (d. 678/1279). Ff. 1–25. Frequently printed at Cairo. Brockelmann I, 451; Suppl. I, 808–9.

2. *Khamrat al-khān wa-rannat al-alḥān*, by 'Abd al-Ghanī b. Ismā'īl al-Nābulusī (d. 1143/1731). Ff. 26–85. Brockelmann, Suppl. I, 811, II, 475.

3. *Nukhabat al-mas'ala fī sharḥ al-Tuḥfat al-mursala*, by the same author. Ff. 86–113. Brockelmann II, 418; Suppl. II, 617.

4. *Marātib al-wujūd*, by Quṭb al-Dīn 'Abd al-Karīm b. Ibrāhīm al-Jīlī (d. 832/1428). Ff. 113–127. Brockelmann II, 206; Suppl. II, 284.

5. *Ḥaqq al-yaqīn wa-zulfat al-tamkīn*, by the same author. Ff. 128–134. Brockelmann II, 206; Suppl. II, 284.

6. *Al-Maurid al-'adhb li-dhawī 'l-wurūd*, by Muḥyī al-Dīn Abū Muḥammad Muṣṭafā b. Kamāl al-Dīn b. 'Alī al-Bakrī al-Ṣiddīqī al-Khalwatī (d. 1162/1749). Ff. 134–147. Brockelmann II, 350; Suppl. II, 477.

7. *Waṣīya*, with commentary of al-Sha'rānī (d. 973/1565), by Abū Isḥāq Ibrāhīm b. 'Alī al-Anṣārī al-Matbūlī (d. 877/1472). Ff. 147–166. Printed at Cairo, 1276/1859. Brockelmann II, 122; Suppl. II, 151.

8. *Kashf al-rān 'an wajh as'ilat al-jānn*. Anonymous, possibly Abu 'l-Mawāhib 'Abd al-Wahhāb b. Aḥmad al-Sha'rānī (d. 973/1565). Ff. 166–216. No other copy appears to be recorded.

Ff. ii+216. Good naskh. 25 Rabī' II 1299/16 March 1882. R. A. Nicholson Bequest.

275 (a) **Or. 1486 (9)**

Al-Qaṣd ilā 'llah, attributed to al-Junaid b. Muḥammad al-Nihāwandī al-Baghdādī (d. 298/910).

Ff. 54. European naskh. Early 14/20th century. (R. A. Nicholson transcript). See *Islamica* II, 402–15. Brockelmann, Suppl. I, 355. R. A. Nicholson Bequest.

276 (a) **Or. 1487 (9)**

1. *Mi'at 'āmil*, by Abū Bakr 'Abd al-Qāhir b. 'Abd al-Raḥmān al-Jurjānī (d. 471/1078). Ff. 1–7. Frequently printed. Brockelmann I, 287; Suppl. I, 503.

2. *Sharḥ Mi'at 'āmil*. Ff. 9–32. Frequently printed. Brockelmann I, 287; Suppl. I, 503.

3. *Risāla fi 'l-jumla*. Ff. 33–38.

4. *Risāla fi 'l-naḥw*. Ff. 41–45.

5. *Al-Miṣbāḥ fi 'l-naḥw*, by Abu'l-Fatḥ Nāṣir b. 'Abd al-Saiyid al-Muṭarrizī (d. 610/1213). Ff. 46–93. Printed at Calcutta, 1803. Brockelmann I, 293; Suppl. I, 514.

Ff. 93. Good naskh. Undated. 12/18th century. R. A. Nicholson Bequest.

277 (a) **Or. 1488 (8)**

Kalīla wa-Dimna, by Abū 'Amr 'Abd Allāh Ibn al-Muqaffa' (Rōzbih b. Dādōe) (d. 142/759).

Ff. 143. Clear naskh. Undated, 12/18th century. Frequently printed. Brockelmann I, 151; Suppl. I, 234. R. A. Nicholson Bequest.

278 (a) **Or. 1489 (8)**

Munyat al-muṣallī wa-ghunyat al-mubtadi', by Sadīd al-Dīn al-Kāshgharī (fl. 7/13th century).

Ff. ii + 106. Clear vocalized naskh. Undated, 11/17th century. Printed several times in India and Turkey. Brockelmann I, 383; Suppl. I, 659. R. A. Nicholson Bequest.

279 (a) **Or. 1490 (11)**

Al-Mukhtaṣar, by Ghars (Ḍiyā') al-Dīn Abu 'l-Ṣafā' Khalīl b. Isḥāq al-Jundī (d. 767/1365).

Ff. 420. Excellent naskh. 8 Sha'bān 1100/28 April 1689. Frequently printed. Brockelmann II, 84; Suppl. II, 96. R. A. Nicholson Bequest.

280 (a) **Or. 1491** (10)

Qur'ān.

Ff. 268. Good naskh. 16 Shauwāl 1069/7 July 1659. Slight illumination on ff. 3*b*–4*a*, margins in red throughout. R. A. Nicholson Bequest.

281 (a) **Or. 1492** (6)

Selections comprising proverbs and verses.

Ff. 34. Good naskh. Undated, 12/18th century. R. A. Nicholson Bequest.

282 (a) **Or. 1493** (7)

Saqṭ al-zand, by Abu 'l-'Alā' Aḥmad b. 'Abd Allāh al-Ma'arrī al-Tanūkhī (d. 449/1057).

Ff. 83. Clear naskh. Undated, 11/17th century. Printed several times at Cairo. Brockelmann I, 254; Suppl. I, 452. R. A. Nicholson Bequest.

283 (a) **Or. 1494** (8)

Risālat al-ghufrān, by Abu 'l-'Alā' al-Ma'arrī.

Ff. 219. Clear scholar's naskh. Undated, 11/17th century. Printed several times at Cairo. Brockelmann I, 256; Suppl. I, 453. R. A. Nicholson Bequest.

284 (a) **Or. 1495** (a)

Al-Tanwīr 'alā Saqṭ al-zand, by Abū Ya'qūb Yūsuf b. Ṭāhir al-Khūwī al-Naḥwī (fl. 532/1137).

Ff. 193. Clear scholar's naskh. Muḥarram 709/June–July 1309. Printed several times at Cairo. Brockelmann, Suppl. I, 453. R. A. Nicholson Bequest.

285 (a) **Or. 1496** (8)

Al-Ḥāwī fī 'ilm al-tadāwī, by Najm al-Dīn Maḥmūd b. Ilyās al-Shīrāzī (d. 730/1330).

Ff. 209. Large, clear naskh. 982/1574–5. Part printed at Beirut, 1902. Brockelmann, Suppl. II, 299. R. A. Nicholson Bequest.

286 (a) **Or. 1497** (8)

Miftāḥ al-ṣudūr fī ḥall alfāẓ Naẓm al-lu'lu' al-manthūr, by 'Ubaid Allāh Maḥmūd b. 'Ubaid Allāh al-Adlabī al-Shāfi'ī (fl. 1090/1679).

Ff. 130. Clear scholar's naskh. 17 Jumādā II 1090/26 June 1679. Holograph. No other copy appears to be recorded. R. A. Nicholson Bequest.

287 (a) **Or. 1498** (7)

Bustān al-adab wa-maḥāsin al-kutub (Part II), by Khalīl b. Aqbughā al-Kamālī (fl. 847/1443).

Ff. 391. Clear scholar's naskh. (Fol. 6*a*) Sha'bān 847/ Nov.–Dec. 1443. Author's holograph draft. No other copy appears to be recorded. R. A. Nicholson Bequest.

288 (a) **Or. 1499** (10)

Murūj al-dhahab, by Abu 'l-Ḥasan 'Alī b. al-Ḥusain al-Mas'ūdī (d. 345/956).

Ff. 382. Excellent naskh. 12 Ṣafar 965/4 Dec. 1557. Printed several times. Brockelmann I, 144; Suppl. I, 220. R. A. Nicholson Bequest.

289 (a) **Or. 1500** (11)

Sharḥ al-Kāfī, by Muḥammad Ṣāliḥ b. Aḥmad al-Māzandarānī (d. 1086/1675).

Ff. 349. Clear ta'līq. 14 Ṣafar 1063/14 Jan. 1653. Brockelmann I, 520. R. A. Nicholson Bequest.

290 (a) **Or. 1501** (8)

Al-Asbāb wa'l-'alāmāt, by Najīb al-Dīn Ḥāmid Muḥammad b. 'Alī b. 'Umar al-Samarqandī (d. 619/1222).

Ff. 219. Clear scholar's naskh. 25 Dhu 'l-Qa'da 887 (?)/ 5 Jan. 1483. Often lithographed in India. Brockelmann I, 489; Suppl. I, 895. R. A. Nicholson Bequest.

291 (a) **Or. 1502** (7)

Ta'līqāt 'ala 'l-Sharḥ al-Muṭauwal, by Muḥammad Farīd b. Muḥammad Sharīf al-Ṣiddīqī al-Aḥmadābādī (fl. 1060/1649).

Ff. 316. Good naskh. Undated, 11/17th century. Brockelmann, Suppl. I, 965. R. A. Nicholson Bequest.

292 (a) **Or. 1503** (8)

Dīwān, by Muḥammad Wafā' al-Shādhilī (d. 765/1363).

Ff. 76. Clear naskh. Undated, 11/17th century. Brockelmann, Suppl. II, 4. R. A. Nicholson Bequest.

293 (a) **Or. 1504 (8)**

Dīwān by Abu 'l-Ṭaiyib Aḥmad b. al-Ḥusain al-Mutanabbī (d. 354/965).

Ff. 205. Good vocalized naskh. 14 Jumādā I 1025/30 May 1616. Frequently printed. Brockelmann I, 86–9; Suppl. I, 138–42. R. A. Nicholson Bequest.

294 (a) **Or. 1505 (10)**

Al-Shāfiya fī sharḥ al-Kāfiya, by Rukn al-Dīn al-Ḥasan b. Muḥammad al-Astarābādī (d. 715/1315).

Ff. 153. Clear naskh. 26 Muḥarram 850/23 April 1446. Printed at Lucknow, 1864. Brockelmann I, 304; Suppl. I, 532. R. A. Nicholson Bequest.

295 (a) **Or. 1506 (8)**

Ta'līq 'alā Risāla fi 'l-ādāb, by Aḥmad b. Muḥammad al-Qāzābādī.

Ff. 62. Good nasta'līq. Undated, 12/18th century. Illuminated 'unwān. No other copy appears to be recorded. R. A. Nicholson Bequest.

296 (a) **Or. 1507 (9)**

Sharḥ Hikmat al-'ain, by Shams al-Dīn Muḥammad b. Mubārakshāh al-Bukhārī al-Harawī (fl. 8/14th century).

Ff. 184. Good naskh. Undated, 11/17th century. Printed several times. Brockelmann I, 466–7; Suppl. I, 847. R. A. Nicholson Bequest.

297 (a) **Or. 1508 (6)**

Al-Lum'at al-nūrānīya fī ḥall mushkilāt al-Shajarat al-Nu'mānīya, by Ṣadr al-Dīn Abu 'l-Ma'ālī Muḥammad b. Isḥāq al-Qūnawī (d. 672/1273).

Ff. 37. Clear scholar's naskh. Undated, 12/18th century. Brockelmann I, 447; Suppl. I, 799. R. A. Nicholson Bequest.

298 (a) **Or. 1509 (8)**

1. *Al-Raḥma fi 'l-ṭibb wa'l-ḥikma*, by Muḥammad b. 'Alī b. Ibrāhīm al-Mahdawī al-Ṣanaubarī al-Yamanī al-Hindī (d. 815/1412). Ff. 1–47*a*. Printed several times. Brockelmann II, 155, 189; Suppl. II, 252.

2. *Urjūza fī 'ilm al-abdān*, by Ibn Sīnā (d. 428/1637). Ff. 47*b*–50. *See* Brockelmann, Suppl. II, 828.

3. A short medical extract and a poem on diet. Ff. 51–52.

4. *Al-Miṣbāḥ fi 'l-adwiyat al-mujarrabat al-ṣiḥāḥ*. Ff. 53–92.

5. *Al-Durrat al-muntakhaba fi 'l-adwiyat al-mujarraba*, by Raḍī al-Dīn Abū Bakr b. Muḥammad al-Fārisī (fl. 700/1300). Ff. 93–141. Brockelmann, Suppl. II, 252.

6. *Mūjibāt al-raḥma wa-'azā'im al-maghfira* [extracts from], by Shihāb al-Dīn Abu 'l-'Abbās Aḥmad b. Abī Bakr b. Muḥammad Ibn al-Raddād al-Qurashī al-Zabīdī (d. 821/1418). Ff. 142–220.

Ff. 220. Clear scholar's naskh. 28 Muḥarram 1151/18 May 1738.

299 (**a**) **Or. 1510 (9)**

1. *Sharḥ al-Ḥizb al-kabīr*, by Abu 'l-Faiḍ Muḥammad Murtaḍa b. Muḥammad al-Ḥusainī al-Zabīdī (d. 1205/1791). Ff. 2–57*a*. Printed at Cairo, 1333/1915. Brockelmann, Suppl. I, 805.

2. *Ḥayāt al-arwāḥ wa-najāt al-ashbāḥ*, by 'Azīz Maḥmūd al-Uskudārī (d. 1037/1628). Brockelmann II, 445; Suppl. II, 661. Ff. 62–111*a*. Followed by various extracts from Ṣadr al-Dīn al-Qūnawī (d. 672/1273), ff. 111*b*–117*a*; a letter in Persian, ff. 117*b*–119*a*; extracts from the *Zubdat al-ḥaqā'iq* of 'Ain al-Quḍāt al-Hamadhānī, ff. 121–137; various other extracts, ff. 137*a*–140; and other short extracts and fragments.

Ff. 157. Excellent naskh and nasta'līq. 1292/1875. R. A. Nicholson Bequest.

300 (**a**) **Or. 1511 (7)**

1. *Al-Risālat al-murshidīya*, by Ṣadr al-Dīn Abu 'l-Ma'ālī Muḥammad b. Isḥāq al-Qūnawī (d. 672/1273). Ff. 1–8. 11/17th century. Brockelmann I, 450; Suppl. I, 808.

2. *Tartīb al-khirqa fī libās al-Ṣūfīya ahl al-khirqa*, by Abū 'Abd Allāh Muḥammad b. Sulaimān b. 'Abd Allāh al-Mu'āfirī al-Shāṭibī (fl. 650/1251). Ff. 11–22*b*. 6 Jumādā I 865/17 Feb. 1461. No other copy appears to be recorded.

3. *Adillat al-firqa fī libās al-khirqa*. Ff. 22*b*–27. No other copy appears to be recorded.

Ff. 30. Two scholars' naskh. R. A. Nicholson Bequest.

301 (a) **Or. 1512 (11)**

Al-Ṭibb al-Manṣūrī, by Abū Bakr Muḥammad b. Zakarīyā' al-Rāzī (d. 313/925).

Ff. 200. Fine old naskh. Rabī' II 579/July-Aug. 1183. Brockelmann I, 234; Suppl. I, 419. R. A. Nicholson Bequest.

302 (a) **Or. 1513 (9)**

Maqāṣid al-'awālī bi-qalā'id al-la'ālī, by Muḥammad b. Muḥammad b. Sulaimān al-Maghribī al-Rūdānī al-Sūsī (d. 1094/1683).

Ff. 80. Clear scholar's naskh. Rajab 1122/Aug.–Sept. 1710. No other copy appears to be recorded. R. A. Nicholson Bequest.

303 (a) **Or. 1514 (12)**

'Arā'is al-bayān fī ḥaqā'iq al-Qur'ān, by Ṣadr al-Dīn Abū Muḥammad Rūzbihān b. Abi 'l-Naṣr al-Baqlī al-Kāzarūnī al-Ṣūfī (d. 606/1209).

Ff. 343. Excellent small naskh. Undated, 10/16th century. Illuminated 'unwān. Lithographed several times in India. Brockelmann I, 414; Suppl. I, 735. R. A. Nicholson Bequest.

304 (a) **Or. 1515 (11)**

Sharḥ Lāmīyat al-'Ajam, by Ṣalāḥ al-Dīn Abu 'l-Ṣafā' Khalīl b. Aibak al-Saifī al-Ṣafadī (d. 764/1363).

Ff. 376. Clear naskh. 17 Muḥarram 1071/22 Sept. 1660. Often printed. Brockelmann I, 247; Suppl. I, 440. R. A. Nicholson Bequest.

305 (a) **Or. 1516 (12)**

Shadharāt al-dhahab fī akhbār man dhahab (second half), by Ibn al-'Imād. *See* no. 264.

Ff. 308. Clear naskh. 27 Rabī' I 1153/25 April 1740. R. A. Nicholson Bequest.

306 (a) **Or. 1517 (8)**

Kanz al-asrār wa-lawāqiḥ al-afkār, by Abū 'Abd Allāh Muḥammad b. Sa'īd b. 'Umar al-Ṣanhājī (fl. 8/14th century).

Ff. 163. Clear ta'līq. 12 Rabī' II 1007/11 Nov. 1598. Brockelmann II, 246; Suppl. II, 344. R. A. Nicholson Bequest.

307 (a) **Or. 1518** (7)

Sulwān al-muṭā' fī 'udwān al-atbā', by Ḥujjat al-Dīn Abū 'Abd Allāh Muḥammad b. 'Abd Allāh Ibn Ẓafar al-Ṣaqalī (d. 565/1169).

Ff. 69. Good scholar's naskh. 819/1416. Printed several times. Brockelmann I, 352; Suppl. I, 595. R. A. Nicholson Bequest.

308 (a) **Or. 1519** (10)

Sulwān al-muṭā', by Ibn Ẓafar. Another copy.

Ff. 155. Excellent naskh. Undated, 10/16th century. R. A. Nicholson Bequest.

309 (a) **Or. 1520** (8)

'Uqūd al-jumān fī akhbār al-zamān, by Muḥammad b. 'Alī al-Shāṭibī al-Maghribī (fl. 890/1465).

Ff. 205. Clear scholar's naskh. Jumādā II 1127/June 1715. Brockelmann II, 263; Suppl. II, 373. R. A. Nicholson Bequest.

310 (a, t) **Or. 1521** (8)

1. *Al-Kibrīt al-aḥmar*, by Ibn 'Arabī (d. 638/1240). Ff. 1–108. Brockelmann, Suppl. II, 659.

2. A Turkish commentary on *Uṣūl al-ḥikam* of Kāfī Ḥasan Efendī al-Āqhiṣārī. Ff. 110–135. Brockelmann, Suppl. I, 792.

3. Part of an untitled work on Muslim religion and ethics. Ff. 138–242.

Ff. 242. Good naskh. Undated, 12/18th century. R. A. Nicholson Bequest.

311 (a) **Or. 1522** (8)

Tāj al-madākhil, by Abū Ja'far Muḥammad b. 'Abd Allāh al-Sharīfī.

Ff. 76. Clear scholar's naskh. Undated, 12/18th century. Diagrams. No other copy appears to be recorded. R. A. Nicholson Bequest.

312 (a) **Or. 1523–4** (10)

Sharḥ Maqāmāt al-Ḥarīrī (vols. I and II), by Aḥmad b. 'Abd al-Mun'im al-Qaisī al-Sharīshī (d. 619/1222).

Ff. 321. Good naskh. 28 Ramaḍān–16 Shauwāl 1247/1–19 March 1832. Printed several times. Brockelmann I, 276; Suppl. I, 487. R. A. Nicholson Bequest.

313 (a) **Or. 1525 (8)**

Sharḥ al-Maqāmāt (vol. I), by al-Sharīshī.

Ff. 277. Clear ta'līq. 28 Ṣafar 1261/8 Mar. 1845. R. A. Nicholson Bequest.

314 (a) **Or. 1526 (9)**

1. *Fatḥ al-wakīl al-kāfī fī sharḥ matn al-Kāfī*, by Aḥmad b. Muḥammad al-Sijā'ī (d. 1190/1777). Ff. 1–60. Dated 19 Ramaḍān 1237/9 June 1822. Brockelmann, Suppl. II, 22.

2. *Al-Qaṣīdat al-Khazrajīya*, by Ḍiyā' al-Dīn Abū Muḥammad 'Abd Allāh b. 'Uthmān al-Khazrajī (fl. 650/1252). Ff. 63–66. Undated, 11/17th century. Often printed. Brockelmann I, 312; Suppl. I, 545.

3. *Fatḥ Rabb al-barīya li-sharḥ al-Qaṣīdat al-Khazrajīya*, by Ibn al-Anṣārī (d. 926/1521). Ff. 67–103. Dated 17 Rabī' I 1188/28 May 1774. Brockelmann I, 312; Suppl. I, 545.

Ff. 103. Three naskh hands. R. A. Nicholson Bequest.

315 (a) **Or. 1527 (8)**

Sharḥ Gulistān, by Muṣliḥ al-Dīn Muṣṭafā b. Sha'bān al-Surūrī (d. 969/1561).

Ff. 236. Clear ta'līq. 9 Ṣafar 1025/27 Feb. 1616. Brockelmann II, 438; Suppl. II, 650. R. A. Nicholson Bequest.

316 (a) **Or. 1528 (12)**

Ḥusn al-muḥāḍara fī akhbār Miṣr wa'l-Qāhira, by Jalāl al-Dīn Abu 'l-Faḍl 'Abd al-Raḥmān b. Abī Bakr b. Muḥammad al-Suyūṭī al-Shāfi'ī (d. 911/1505).

Ff. 353. Clear naskh. 18 Ramaḍān 1085/16 Dec. 1674. Printed several times in Cairo. Brockelmann II, 157; Suppl. II, 196. R. A. Nicholson Bequest.

317 (a) **Or. 1529 (8)**

Ḥusn al-muḥāḍara fī akhbār Miṣr wa'l-Qāhira, by al-Suyūṭī. Another copy.

Ff. 297. Clear scholar's naskh. 15 Ramaḍān 993/10 Sept. 1585. R. A. Nicholson Bequest.

318 (**a**) **Or. 1530** (**8**)

Ḥusn al-muḥāḍara fī akhbār Miṣr wa'l-Qāhira, by al-Suyūṭī. Another copy.

Ff. 227. Clear scholar's naskh. 2 Shauwāl 1011/25 March 1603. R. A. Nicholson Bequest.

319 (**a**) **Or. 1531** (**8**)

Al-Maqāmāt, by al-Suyūṭī.

Ff. 53. Clear scholar's naskh. Undated, 11/17th century. Printed several times. Brockelmann II, 158; Suppl. II, 197. R. A. Nicholson Bequest.

320 (**a**) **Or. 1532** (**8**)

1. A fragment of a treatise on magic. Ff. 1–54.
2. *Al-Tathbīt 'inda 'l-tabyīt*, by Jalāl al-Dīn Abu 'l-Faḍl 'Abd al-Raḥmān b. Abī Bakr al-Suyūṭī (d. 911/1505). Ff. 59–67. Printed several times at Fez. Brockelmann II, 151; Suppl. II, 187.
3. *Su'āl ba'ḍ ahl al-dhimma*, by Taqī al-Dīn Abu 'l-'Abbās Aḥmad b. 'Abd al-Ḥalīm Ibn Taimīya al-Ḥarrānī (d. 682/1283). Ff. 69–76*a*. Printed at Cairo, 1906. Brockelmann, Suppl. II, 125.
4. *Al-Nuṣūṣ fī taḥqīq al-ṭaur al-makhṣūṣ*, by Ṣadr al-Dīn al-Qūnawī (d. 672/1273). Ff. 79–118. Printed at Teheran, 1315/1897. Brockelmann I, 450; Suppl. I, 807.

Ff. 121. Clear scholar's naskh. Undated, 10/16th century. R. A. Nicholson Bequest.

321 (**a**) **Or. 1533** (**8**)

'Uqūd al-jumān fī 'ilm al-ma'ānī wa'l-bayān, by Jalāl al-Dīn al-Suyūṭī (d. 911/1505).

Ff. 80. Small, clear naskh. 25 Rajab 1026/29 July 1617. Printed several times. Brockelmann I, 295; Suppl. I, 519. R. A. Nicholson Bequest.

322 (**a**) **Or. 1534** (**9**)

Sharḥ al-Mu'allaqāt, by Abū Zakarīyā' Yaḥyā b. 'Alī Ibn al-Khaṭīb al-Tibrīzī (d. 502/1109).

Ff. 208. Clear naskh. Undated, 12/18th century. Printed several times. Brockelmann I, 18; Suppl. I, 35. R. A. Nicholson Bequest.

323 (a) **Or. 1535 (9)**

Al-Sharḥ al-Muṭauwal, by Sa'd al-Dīn Mas'ūd b. 'Umar al-Taftazānī (d. 792/1390).

Ff. 240. Good ta'līq. Undated, 11/17th century. Illuminated 'unwān; margins ruled in gold and black. Often printed. Brockelmann I, 294; Suppl. I, 516. R. A. Nicholson bequest.

324 (a) **Or. 1536 (8)**

Sharḥ al-Mukhtaṣar (*al-'Aqā'id lil-Nasafī*), by Sa'd al-Dīn al-Taftazānī.

Ff. 99. Good maghribī. Undated, 11/17th century. Printed several times. Brockelmann I, 427; Suppl. I, 758–9. R. A. Nicholson Bequest.

325 (a) **Or. 1537 (8)**

Yawāqīt al-mawāqīt, by Abū Manṣūr 'Abd al-Malik b. Muḥammad b. Ismā'īl al-Tha'ālibī (d. 429/1038).

Ff. 73. Good naskh. 5 Rabī' II 1156/29 May 1743. Printed several times. Brockelmann I, 286; Suppl. I, 501. R. A. Nicholson Bequest.

326 (a) **Or. 1538 (8)**

Ghurar al-balāgha, by Abū Manṣūr al-Tha'ālibī.

Ff. 70. Good scholar's naskh. 13 Rabī' II 1118/25 July 1706. Brockelmann I, 285; Suppl. I, 500. R. A. Nicholson Bequest.

327 (a) **Or. 1539 (12)**

Sharḥ Dīwān al-Mutanabbī, by Abu 'l-Ḥasan 'Alī b. Aḥmad b. Muḥammad al-Wāḥidī al-Nīsābūrī (d. 468/1075).

Ff. 301. Excellent naskh. Rabī' II 1112/Sept.–Oct. 1700. Printed several times. Brockelmann I, 88; Suppl. I, 142. R. A. Nicholson Bequest.

328 (a) **Or. 1540 (9)**

Ta'līqāt 'ala 'l-Sharḥ al-Mukhtaṣar, by Yāsīn b. Zain al-Dīn al-'Alīmī al-Ḥimṣī (d. 1061/1651).

Ff. 217. Clear maghribī. Jumādā II 1136/March 1724. Brockelmann I, 295; Suppl. I, 518. R. A. Nicholson Bequest.

329 (a) **Or. 1541** (9)

Al-Mufaṣṣal, by Abu 'l-Qāsim Maḥmūd b. 'Umar al-Zamakhsharī (d. 538/1144).

Ff. 132. Clear naskh. Dhu 'l-Ḥijja 1140/July 1728. Printed several times. Brockelmann I, 291; Suppl. I, 509. R. A. Nicholson Bequest.

330 (a) **Or. 1542** (6)

Sharḥ Ta'līm al-muta'allim, by Ibrāhīm b. Ismā'īl (fl. 996/1585).

Ff. 10. Clear ta'līq. 1 Rabī' I 1011/19 Aug. 1602. Printed several times. Brockelmann, Suppl. I, 837. R. A. Nicholson Bequest.

331 (a) **Or. 1543** (8)

Elegant extracts by 'Aqīl al-Raushanī al-Ḥalabī (fl. 1850).

Ff. 128. Clear naskh. Undated, 13/19th century. No other copy appears to be recorded, possibly holograph. R. A. Nicholson Bequest.

332 (p) **Or. 1544** (9)

Four anonymous treatises on Arabic grammar.

Ff. 72. Clear nasta'līq. Undated, 12/18th century. R. A. Nicholson Bequest.

333 (a) **Or. 1545** (6)

Al-Ajwibat al-jalīya fi 'l-uṣūl al-'Arabīya (*al-naḥwīya*), by Muḥammad Bey Talḥūq.

Ff. 116. Clear naskh. 9 September 1771. Printed frequently. Brockelmann, Suppl. II, 332. R. A. Nicholson Bequest.

334 (a) **Or. 1546** (10)

Al-Shāmil (a large fragment), by 'Alā' al-Dīn Abu 'l-Ḥasan 'Alī b. Abi 'l-Ḥazm Ibn al-Nafīs al-Qurashī (d. 687/1288).

Ff. 178. Scholar's cursive naskh. Undated, 8/14th century. *See* Brockelmann, Suppl. I, 900. R. A. Nicholson Bequest.

335 (a) **Or. 1547** (6)

1. *Dalā'il al-khairāt*, by Abū 'Abd Allāh Muḥammad b. Sulaimān b. Abī Bakr al-Juzūlī al-Simlālī (d. 870/1465).

Ff. 1–82. Frequently printed. Brockelmann II, 253; Suppl. II, 359.

2. *Al-Ḥiṣn al-haṣīn min kalām Saiyid al-mursalīn*, by Shams al-Dīn Abu 'l-Khair Muḥammad b. Muḥammad al-Jazarī al-Qurashī al-Dimashqī al-Shīrāzī (d. 833/1429). Ff. 83–144. Printed many times. Brockelmann II, 203; Suppl. II, 277.

3. *Qaṣīdat al-Burda*, by Sharaf al-Dīn Abū 'Abd Allāh al-Būṣīrī (d. 694/1296). Ff. 145–152. *See* no. 78.

4. *Al-Ḥizb al-kabīr*, by Nūr al-Dīn Abu 'l-Ḥasan Aḥmad b. 'Abd Allāh b. 'Abd al-Jabbār al-Ḥasanī al-Idrīsī al-Mi'mārī al-Shādhilī al-Zarwīlī (d. 656/1258). Ff. 153–159. Brockelmann I, 449; Suppl. I, 805.

5. *Ṣalāt*, by Abū Muḥammad 'Abd al-Salām Ibn Mashīsh b. Abī Bakr al-Ḥasanī al-Idrīsī al-Kāmilī (d. 625/1228). Ff. 160–161 *a*[1]. Printed at Istanbul, 1256/1840. Brockelmann I, 440; Suppl. I, 788.

6. *Ḥizb al-baḥr*, by al-Shādhilī (d. 656/1258). Ff. 161 *a*[5]–163 *a*; followed by an anonymous prayer, ff. 163 *b*–164. Often printed. Brockelmann I, 449; Suppl. I, 805.

Ff. 167. Good maghribī. 12/18th century. Some illumination throughout. R. A. Nicholson Bequest.

336 (a) **Or. 1548 (8)**

An anthology of Arabic poetry in the form of a Bayāḍ.

Ff. 100. Good naskh. Undated, 12/18th century. Coloured 'unwān on fol. 1 *b*. R. A. Nicholson Bequest.

337 (a) **Or. 1549 (8)**

An anthology of poetry.

Ff. 166. Clear naskh. Undated, 12/18th century. 'Unwān, margins ruled in gold and black throughout. R. A. Nicholson Bequest.

338 (a) **Or. 1550 (11)**

Yatīmat al-dahr fī maḥāsin ahl al-'aṣr, by Abū Manṣūr al-Tha'ālibī (d. 429/1038).

Ff. 370. Excellent naskh. Undated, 12/18th century. Printed at Damascus, 1304/1887, Cairo, 1934. Brockelmann I, 284; Suppl. I, 499. R. A. Nicholson Bequest.

339 (a) **Or. 1551** (8)

1. *Ḥikmat al-ishrāq*, by Shihāb al-Dīn Abu 'l-Futūḥ Aḥmad b. Ḥabash b. Amīrak al-Suhrawardī al-Maqtūl (d. 587/1191). Ff. 1–57. Printed twice in Persia. Brockelmann I, 437; Suppl. I, 782.

2. *Al-Nafaḥāt al-Ilāhīya*, by Ṣadr al-Dīn al-Qūnawī (d. 672/1273). Ff. 58–63. Brockelmann I, 450; Suppl. I, 807.

3. *Al-Isfār al-gharīb natījat al-safar al-qarīb*, by Quṭb al-Dīn 'Abd al-Karīm b. Ibrāhīm al-Jīlī (d. 826/1423). Ff. 65–69. Brockelmann II, 206.

4. *Tuḥfat al-aḥrār fī bayān kashf sirr al-asrār*, by Ḥasan b. Muḥammad b. Ḥamza al-Shīrāzī al-Balāsī (fl. 700/1300). Ff. 71–152. Brockelmann, Suppl. II, 1003.

Ff. 152. Clear scholar's naskh. 9/15th century. R. A. Nicholson Bequest.

340 (a) **Or. 1552** (8)

Sīrat 'Antar b. Shaddād (extract).

Ff. 58. Clear naskh. 12/18th century. Printed several times. Brockelmann II, 62; Suppl. II, 64. R. A. Nicholson Bequest.

341 (a) **Or. 1553** (7)

Portions of the *Qur'ān*, and magical scraps.

Ff. 102. West African hand. 12/18th century. Loose, within rough leather boards. R. A. Nicholson Bequest.

340 (a) **Or. 1554** (13)

A treatise on medicine, imperfect at the beginning.

Ff. 97. Excellent naskh. 28 Dhu 'l-Qa'da 703/2 July 1304. R. A. Nicholson Bequest.

343 (p) **Or. 1555** (9)

Sharḥ-i Mathnawī-yi ma'nawī (Daftars 4–6).

Ff. 193. Clear nasta'līq. 3 Jumādā II of fifth year of Aḥmad Shah's reign, i.e. 1166/7 April 1753. *See* Ivanow 505–17. R. A. Nicholson Bequest.

344 (p) **Or. 1556** (8)

Dīwān, by Abū Naṣr Aḥmad b. Abi 'l-Ḥasan Nāmiqī Jāmī, called Aḥmad-i Jām (d. 536/1142).

Ff. 64. Clear nasta'līq. 11/17th century. Ivanow 436. R. A. Nicholson Bequest.

345 (p) **Or. 1557 (9)**

Daqā'iq al-ḥaqā'iq, by Aḥmad Rūmī (fl. 700/1297).

Ff. 226. Clear nasta'līq. 14 Rabī' I of 13th year of Muḥammad Shāh, i.e. 1144/16 Sept. 1731. Ivanow 1187. R. A. Nicholson Bequest.

346 (p) **Or. 1558 (11)**

Ikhtiyārāt-i Badī'ī, by 'Alī b. Ḥusain al-Anṣārī Ḥajji Zain al-'Aṭṭār (d. 806/1404).

Ff. 255. Clear nasta'līq. 11/17th century. Lithographed at Cawnpore, 1879. Ivanow-Curzon 588. R. A. Nicholson Bequest.

347 (p) **Or. 1559 (12)**

Kullīyāt, by Yamīn al-Dīn Abu 'l-Ḥasan Amīr Khusrau Dihlawī (d. 725/1325).

Ff. 521. Excellent nasta'līq. 12/18th century. Fully illuminated opening pages; margins ruled throughout in gold and colours. Ethé, I.O. 1186. R. A. Nicholson Bequest.

348 (p) **Or. 1560 (10)**

Nāmūs-i akbar, by Ḍiyā' al-Dīn Nakhshabī (d. *ca.* 750/1350).

Ff. 135. Clear nasta'līq. 9 Shauwāl 1123/19 Nov. 1711. Ivanow 335. R. A. Nicholson Bequest.

349 (p) **Or. 1561–2 (8)**

Dabistān, by (?) Mūbad Shāh (fl. 1065/1655).

Ff. 156+114. Good nasta'līq. Rabī' II, 1245/Oct. 1829. Printed frequently. Ethé, I.O. 2542, Ivanow 1134. R. A. Nicholson Bequest.

350 (p) **Or. 1563 (12)**

Tarjamat al-Faraj ba'd al-shidda, by Ḥusain b. As'ad Dihistānī Mu'aiyadī (fl. 6/12th century). *See* no. 61.

Ff. 341. Clear nasta'līq. 12/18th century. R. A. Nicholson Bequest.

351 (p) **Or. 1564 (7)**

Tamhīdāt, by Abu 'l-Ma'āli 'Abd Allāh b. Muḥammad 'Ain al-Quḍāt al-Hamadhānī (d. 533/1138).

Ff. 149. Excellent nasta'līq. 10/16th century. Ivanow 1166. R. A. Nicholson Bequest.

352 (p) **Or. 1565 (8)**

An acephalous treatise on medicine.

Ff. 123. Excellent nasta'līq. 803/1400. R. A. Nicholson Bequest.

353 (p) **Or. 1566 (8)**

Dīwān, by Jāmī (d. 898/1492).

Ff. 140. Excellent nasta'līq. Early 10/16th century. Fine 'unwān, gilt and black margins throughout. Printed several times. Ivanow 612 (25). R. A. Nicholson Bequest.

354 (p) **Or. 1567 (9)**

Dīwān, by Jāmī. Another copy.

Ff. 184. Clear nasta'līq. 11/17th century. Fine 'unwān, gilt and black margins throughout. R. A. Nicholson Bequest.

355 (p) **Or. 1568 (8)**

Tuḥfat al-'Irāqain, by Khāqānī (d. *ca.* 595/1199). *See* no. 168 (1).

Ff. 113. Clear nasta'līq. Undated 12/18th century. R. A. Nicholson Bequest.

356 (p) **Or. 1569 (10)**

Nūr al-'uyūn, by Abū Rūḥ Muḥammad b. Manṣūr al-Jurjānī called Zarrīn-Dast (fl. 480/1090).

Ff. 321. Clear nasta'līq. 14 Rajab 1130/13 June 1718. Ivanow 1529. R. A. Nicholson Bequest.

357 (p) **Or. 1570 (11)**

Tuḥfat al-mu'minīn, by Muḥammad Mu'min b. Mīr Muḥammad Zamān Tankābunī Dailamī (fl. 1100/1599).

Ff. 378. Rather cursive nasta'līq. Undated, 12/18th century. Ivanow 1562. R. A. Nicholson Bequest.

358 (p) **Or. 1571 (13)**

Tuḥfat al-mu'minīn, by Muḥammad Mu'min. Another copy.

Ff. 223. Clear nasta'līq. 5 Jumādā II 1195/29 May 1781. R. A. Nicholson Bequest.

359 (p) **Or. 1572 (10)**

Khamsa, by Jamāl al-Dīn Abū Muḥammad Ilyās b. Yūsuf Niẓāmī (d. *ca.* 600/1204).

Ff. 306. Good nasta'līq. 1019/1610–11. Decorated 'unwāns; margins in gold and colours throughout. Many times lithographed. Ivanow 466. R. A. Nicholson Bequest.

360 (p) **Or. 1573–4 (11)**

Ẓafar-nāma, by Niẓām al-Dīn 'Abd al-Wāsi' Shāmī (fl. 804/1402).

Ff. 402. Clear naskh. 1912. Printed (ed. F. Tauer), Prague, 1937. Storey, p. 279, no. 354. R. A. Nicholson Bequest.

361 (p) **Or. 1575 (9)**

Fawā'id-i bāhiya, by Ḥasan b. 'Alī al-Ṭaiyib.

Ff. 70. Excellent nasta'līq. 12/18th century. R. A. Nicholson Bequest.

362 (p) **Or. 1576 (7)**

Qarābādīn-i Yūsufī, by Yūsuf b. Muḥammad b. Yūsuf called Yūsufī (fl. 940/1532).

Ff. 41. Excellent nasta'līq. 11/17th century. Decorated 'unwān. R. A. Nicholson Bequest.

363 (p) **Or. 1577 (11)**

Jāmi' al-tawārīkh (portions), by Rashīd al-Dīn Faḍl Allāh b. 'Imād al-Daula Hamadhānī (d. 718/1318).

Ff. 211. Excellent nasta'līq. 13/19th century. Storey, p. 72, no. 106. R. A. Nicholson Bequest.

364 (p) **Or. 1578 (11)**

Fīhi mā fīhi, by Jalāl al-Dīn Rūmī.

Ff. 120. Clear naskh. 23 Jumādā I 1342/1 Jan. 1924. Lithographed at Teheran and Azamgarh. Ivanow-Curzon 417. R. A. Nicholson Bequest.

365 (p) **Or. 1579 (9)**

Fīhi mā fīhi, by Jalāl al-Dīn Rūmī. Another copy.

Ff. 117. European naskh. *ca.* 1935. R. A. Nicholson's own transcription of a transcript of a copy in the Hyderabad State Library. R. A. Nicholson Bequest.

366 (p) **Or. 1580 (10)**

Mathnawī-yi ma'nawī, by Jalāl al-Dīn Rūmī. *See* no. 35.

Ff. 341. Clear ta'līq. 843/1439–40. Decorated 'unwān; margins in gold and colour throughout. R. A. Nicholson Bequest.

367 (p) **Or. 1581 (8)**

Gulistān, by Sa'dī (d. 691/1292).

Ff. 178. Good nasta'līq. 8 October 1820. Frequently printed. Ivanow 532. R. A. Nicholson Bequest.

368 (p) **Or. 1582 (12)**

Kullīyāt, by Sa'dī.

Ff. 236. Good nasta'līq. 997/1588–9. Fully illuminated opening pages, vignettes and coloured margins throughout. Often lithographed. Ethé, I.O. 1117. R. A. Nicholson Bequest.

369 (p) **Or. 1583 (7)**

Tuḥfa-yi Sāmī, by Sām Mīrzā (d. 984/1576). *See* no. 184.

Ff. 146. Clear nasta'līq. 2 Jumādā II 987/27 July 1579. 'Unwān. R. A. Nicholson Bequest.

370 (p) **Or. 1584 (9)**

Ḥadīqat al-ḥaqīqa, by Abu 'l-Majd Majdūd b. Ādam Sanā'ī (d. *ca.* 545/1150).

Ff. 313. Clear nasta'līq. 1004/1595–6. Good 'unwān. Frequently lithographed in India; printed at Teheran, 1329/1950. Ivanow 438 (4). R. A. Nicholson Bequest.

371 (p) **Or. 1585 (10)**

Kashf al-lughāt wa'l-iṣṭilāḥāt, by 'Abd al-Raḥīm b. Aḥmad Sūr (fl. 950/1543).

Ff. 412. Clear nasta'līq. 21 Rabī' II 1224/5 June 1809. Printed at Calcutta, 1264/1847. Ivanow 1416. R. A. Nicholson Bequest.

372 (p) **Or. 1586 (9)**

Nafaḥāt al-uns, by Jāmī. *See* no. 94.

Ff. 452. Clear nasta'līq. 11/17th century. 'Unwān, margins ruled throughout in gold and blue. R. A. Nicholson Bequest.

373 (p) **Or. 1587 (9)**

Daqā'iq al-inshā', by Ranjhūr Dās (fl. 1145/1732).

Ff. 107. Good nasta'līq. 12/18th century. Ethé, I.O. 2120. R. A. Nicholson Bequest.

374 (p) **Or. 1588** (14)

Diploma appointing Professor R. A. Nicholson a member of the Persian Academy.

Ff. 2. Calligraphic nasta'līq. 26/8/1322/1944. Fully illuminated. Lacquer covers. R. A. Nicholson Bequest.

375 (a) **Or. 1596** (5)

A collection of prayers.

Ff. 112. Calligraphic naskh. 12/18th century. 'Unwān, margins ruled in gold and black. Presented by W. S. Adie.

376 (a) **Or. 1597** (9)

Prayers, etc.

Ff. 38. Calligraphic naskh. 12/18th century. 'Unwān, margins ruled in gold and red. Presented by W. S. Adie.

377 (a) **Or. 1598** (7)

al-Ṣaḥīfat al-kāmila, attributed to Zain al-'Ābidīn 'Alī b. al-Ḥusain al-Sajjād (d. 92/710). *See* no. 48.

Ff. 128. Calligraphic naskh. 12/18th century. 'Unwān, margins ruled in gold, blue and black. Presented by W. S. Adie.

378 (a) **Or. 1599** (5)

al-Ṣaḥīfat al-kāmila, by Zain al-'Ābidīn. Another copy.

Ff. 210. Calligraphic naskh. Dhu 'l-Ḥijja 1078/May 1668. Illuminated 'unwān, margins ruled in gold and colours. Presented by W. S. Adie.

379 (a) **Or. 1600** (5)

al-Ṣaḥīfat al-kāmila, by Zain al-'Ābidīn. Another copy.

Ff. 179. Clear naskh. 12/18th century. 'Unwān, margins ruled in gold, black and blue. Presented by W. S. Adie.

380 (a) **Or. 1601** (3)

Qur'ān (miniature copy).

Ff. 398. Calligraphic naskh. 1104/1692–3. Lacquered boards. Presented by W. S. Adie.

381 (a) **Or. 1602** (4)

Qur'ān (miniature copy).

Ff. 336. Calligraphic naskh. 1122/1710–11. Presented by W. S. Adie.

382 (a) **Or. 1603** (4)

Qur'ān (miniature copy).

Ff. 586. Calligraphic naskh. 12/18th century. Presented by W. S. Adie.

383 (a) **Or. 1604** (4)

Qur'ān (Sūras 17–25).

Ff. 136. Calligraphic naskh. 12/18th century. Presented by W. S. Adie.

384 (a) **Or. 1605** (4)

Qur'ān (miniature copy).

Ff. 363. Calligraphic naskh. 12/18th century. Presented by W. S. Adie.

385 (a) **Or. 1606** (5)

Qur'ān.

Ff. 214. Small calligraphic naskh. 12/18th century. Presented by W. S. Adie.

386 (a) **Or. 1607** (6)

Qur'ān.

Ff. 571. Calligraphic naskh. 11/17th century. Presented by W. S. Adie.

387 (a) **Or. 1608** (6)

Qur'ān.

Ff. 360. Calligraphic naskh. 11/17th century. Presented by W. S. Adie.

388 (a) **Or. 1609** (8)

Qur'ān (selected Sūras).

Ff. 39. Calligraphic naskh. 12/18th century. Inscribed in gold. Presented by W. S. Adie.

389 (a) **Or. 1610** (9)

Qur'ān.

Ff. 281. Calligraphic naskh. 11/17th century. Presented by W. S. Adie.

390 (a) **Or. 1611** (9)

Qur'ān.

Ff. 472. Calligraphic naskh. 12/18th century. Presented by W. S. Adie.

391 (**a**) **Or. 1612** (**9**)

Qur'ān.

Ff. 342. Calligraphic naskh. 12/18th century. Presented by W. S. Adie.

392 (**a, p**) **Or. 1613** (**6**)

Selected Sūras from the *Qur'ān*, prayers, etc.

Ff. 161. Clear naskh. Jumādā II 1219/Sept. 1804. Presented by W. S. Adie.

393 (**a**) **Or. 1614** (**7**)

Qur'ān, with interlineary Persian translation.

Ff. 257. Calligraphic naskh and nasta'līq. 12/18th century. Presented by W. S. Adie.

394 (**a, p**) **Or. 1615** (**9**)

Qur'ān (selected Sūras) with Persian interlineary translation.

Ff. 67. Calligraphic naskh. 12/18th century. Presented by W. S. Adie.

395 (**a, p**) **Or. 1616** (**10**)

Qur'ān, with Persian interlineary translation.

Ff. 554. Calligraphic naskh and nasta'līq. 12/18th century. Presented by W. S. Adie.

396 (**a, p**) **Or. 1617** (**15**)

Qur'ān, with Persian interlineary translation and marginal notes.

Ff. 417. Calligraphic naskh. 12/18th century. Fully illuminated opening pages, margins ruled in gold and colour throughout. Presented by W. S. Adie.

397 (**a, p**) **Or. 1618** (**9**)

Prayers.

Ff. 35. Calligraphic naskh. 12/18th century. Illuminated 'unwān, margins ruled in gold, black and blue. Presented by W. S. Adie.

398 (**a, p**) **Or. 1619** (**7**)

Al-Ṣaḥīfat al-kāmila, by Zain al-'Ābidīn, with Persian interlineary translation. *See* no. 48.

Ff. 327. Calligraphic naskh and nasta‘līq. 12/18th century. Margins ruled in gold, black and blue. Presented by W. S. Adie.

399 (a, p) **Or. 1620 (6)**

Prayers, etc.

Ff. 65. Naskh. 12/18th century. Presented by W. S. Adie.

400 (p) **Or. 1622 (5)**

Dīwān, by Ḥāfiẓ. *See* no. 40.

Ff. 226. Calligraphic nasta‘līq. 7 Rabī‘ I 1070/22 Nov. 1659. Illuminated ‘unwān, margins ruled in gold, black and blue. Presented by W. S. Adie.

401 (p) **Or. 1623 (8)**

Mathnawī (Daftars 2–4), by Jalāl al-Dīn Rūmī. *See* no. 35.

Ff. 484. Calligraphic naskh. 11/17th century. ‘Unwāns, vignettes, margins ruled in gold and black. Presented by W. S. Adie.

402 (p) **Or. 1624 (8)**

Jāmi‘-i ‘Abbāsī, by Bahā’ al-Dīn Muḥammad b. al-Ḥusain al-‘Āmilī (d. 1031/1622).

Ff. 271. Clear nasta‘līq. 12/18th century. Ivanow 1112. Presented by W. S. Adie.

403 (p) **Or. 1625 (8)**

Kullīyāt, by Sa‘dī. *See* no. 368.

Ff. 107. Calligraphic nasta‘līq. 11/17th century. Presented by W. S. Adie.

404 (p) **Or. 1626 (8)**

Kullīyāt, by Sa‘di. Another copy.

Ff. 352. Clear nasta‘līq. 12/18th century. Presented by W. S. Adie.

405 (a, p) **Or. 1627 (8)**

Sharḥ Khulāṣat al-ḥisāb.

Ff. 219. Clear nasta‘līq. 12/18th century. *See* Brockelmann II, 415; Suppl. II, 596. Presented by W. S. Adie.

406 (p) **Or. 1628 (9)**

Qiṣṣa-yi Kāmrūp, by Muḥammad Kāẓim Ḥusainī Karīm (fl. 1035/1626).

Ff. 184. Clear nasta'līq. 12/18th century. 'Unwān and margins ruled, numerous miniatures. Lithographed at Delhi, 1849. Ethé, I.O. 821. Presented by W. S. Adie.

407 (a, p) **Or. 1629 (9)**

Prayers.

Ff. 155. Clear shikasta. 12/18th century. Presented by W. S. Adie.

408 (p) **Or. 1630 (9)**

Mathnawī (part), by Jalāl al-Dīn Rūmī. *See* no. 35.

Ff. 99. Calligraphic nasta'līq. 10/16th century. Presented by W. S. Adie.

409 (p) **Or. 1631 (9)**

Sharḥ-i Niṣāb al-ṣibyān.

Ff. 128. Clear nasta'līq. 12/18th century. Presented by W. S. Adie.

410 (p) **Or. 1632 (10)**

Four tracts on calligraphy.

Ff. 178. Clear nasta'līq. 1126/1714. Presented by W. S. Adie.

411 (p) **Or. 1633 (11)**

Fragment of a Persian manuscript.

Ff. 275. Clear nasta'līq. 12/18th century. Presented by W. S. Adie.

412 (p) **Or. 1634 (12)**

'Ain al-ḥayāt (vol. 1), by Muḥammad Bāqir b. Muḥammad Taqī Majlisī. *See* no. 52.

Ff. 318. Clear nasta'līq. 1149/1736–7. Presented by W. S. Adie.

413 (p) **Or. 1635 (11)**

Risāla-yi ṣaidīya, and other tracts, by Muḥammad 'Alī Ḥazīn (d. 1180/1766).

Ff. 77. Clear nasta'līq. 3 Rabī' 1 1236/9 Dec. 1820. Presented by W. S. Adie.

414 (a) **Or. 1639** (**8**)

Laṭā'if al-azal, by Ṣubḥ-i Azal (d. 1911).

Ff. 102. Clear naskh. Holograph. [1910]. No other copy appears to be recorded. Presented by Mrs M. B. Thorne.

415 (p) **Or. 1662** (**7**)

Fārs-nāma, by Ibn al-Balkhī (fl. 500/1119). [Photostats of Paris MS.]

Ff. 170. Clear nasta'līq. 1273/1856. Printed at London, 1921 (ed. by G. Le Strange and R. A. Nicholson). Storey, p. 350, no. 458. R. A. Nicholson Bequest.

416 (p) **Or. 1663** (**8**)

Fārs-nāma, by Ibn al-Balkhī. [Photostats of British Museum MS.]

Ff. 180. Clear naskh. 8/14th century. R. A. Nicholson Bequest.

417 (a) **Or. 1664** (**9**)

al-'Ilm al-muktasab fī zirā'at al-dhahab, by Abu 'l-Qāsim Muḥammad b. Aḥmad al-'Irāqī al-Sīmāwī (fl. 6/12th century). [Photostats of Paris MS. 2611.]

Ff. 57. Brockelmann I, 497; Suppl. I, 909. R. A. Nicholson Bequest.

418 (a) **Or. 1665** (**9**)

Al-Ṭilasmāt, by Abū Bakr Muḥammad (Aḥmad) b. 'Alī Ibn Waḥshīya al-Nabaṭī (fl. 3/9 century). [Photostats of Bodleian MS. Hunt 75.]

Ff. 131. Clear naskh. 971/1563. Brockelmann I, 243. R. A. Nicholson Bequest.

419 (a) **Or. 1666** (**7**)

Al-Muktasab fī 'ilm al-kāf. [Photostats of British Museum MS. Or. 3751, ff. 30–76.]

Ff. 48. Clear naskh. R. A. Nicholson Bequest.

420 (p) **Or. 1667–9** (**7**)

Walad-nāma, by Bahā'al-Dīn Aḥmad Sulṭān Walad b. Jalāl al-Dīn Rūmī (d. 712/1313). [Photographs of MS. Nafiz Pasha 480.]

Ff. 80+101+80. Clear naskh. Printed at Teheran, 1316/1937. Ivanow 547. R. A. Nicholson Bequest.

421 (p) **Or. 1670–1 (8)**

1. *Dīwān.*
2. *Mukhtār-nāma.*
3. *Hailāj-nāma.* All by Farīd al-Dīn Abū Ḥāmid Muḥammad b. Abī Bakr Ibrāhīm Nīshāpūrī 'Aṭṭār (d. *ca.* 620/1223). [Photostats of MS in possession of C. P. Skrine.]

Ff. 247+206. Excellent ta'līq. 9/15th century. Lithographed at Lucknow, 1872. Ivanow 477. R. A. Nicholson Bequest.

422 (p) **Or. 1672 (12)**

1. *Fīhi mā fīhi*, by Jalāl al-Dīn Rūmī. *See* no. 364.
2. *Ṭarab al-majālis*, by Fakhr al-Sādāt Rukn al-Dīn Ḥusain b. 'Ālim Ḥusainī (d. *ca.* 730/1330). Ethé, I.O. 1829. [Photographs of Skrine MS.]

Ff. 106. 9/15th century. R. A. Nicholson Bequest.

423 (a) **Or. 1673 (8)**

al-Luma', by Abū Naṣr 'Abd Allāh b. 'Alī b. Muḥammad al-Sarrāj (d. 378/988). [Photostats of British Museum MS. Or. 7710.]

Ff. 241. Clear naskh. 548/1153. Edited (R. A. Nicholson) London, 1914. Brockelmann, Suppl. I, 359. R. A. Nicholson Bequest.

424 (a) **Or. 1674 (6)**

al-Luma', by Abū Naṣr al-Sarrāj. [Photographs of ff. 157–168 of the Bankipore MS.]

Ff. 12. Old naskh. Edited (A. J. Arberry) London, 1947. R. A. Nicholson Bequest.

425 (a) **Or. 1675 (10)**

al-Luma', by Abū Naṣr al-Sarrāj. [Portion transcribed by R. A. Nicholson from the Bankipore MS.]

Ff. 24. Modern European naskh. *ca.* 1935. R. A. Nicholson Bequest.

426 (p) **Or. 1676 (9)**

Silsilat al-dhahab, by Jāmī. [Photograph of MS. in possession of Prof. D. S. Robertson.]

Ff. 83. Clear ta'līq. 884/1479. Printed and lithographed several times. Ivanow 612 (17). Presented by Prof. D. S. Robertson.

427 (p) **Or. 1679 (8)**

1. *Subḥat al-abrār*, by Jāmī. *See* no. 33.

2. *'Arūḍ-i Jāmī*, by Jāmī. Edited (by H. Blochmann), Calcutta, 1872. Ivanow 612 (9).

3. *Dīwān-i Kalīm*, by Abū Ṭālib Hamadānī Kalīm (d. 1062/1652). Lithographed several times. Ivanow 754.

Ff. 276. Three clear nasta'līq hands. (1) 20 Ramaḍān 1049/15 Jan. 1640; (2) 11/17th century; (3) 12/18th century.

428 (a) **Or. 1680 (8)**

Dīwān, by Muḥammad 'Alī Iṣfahānī Ṣā'ib (d. 1088/1677).

Ff. 224. Clear ta'līq. 24 Ramaḍān 1156/11 Nov. 1743. Gold 'unwān, margins ruled throughout in red. Lithographed several times. Ivanow 783.

429 (p) **Or. 1681 (8)**

Calendar for the year 1303/1885.

Ff. 16. Clear naskh and nasta'līq. 1304/1886. Some illumination.

430 (p) **Or. 1682 (8)**

Yūsuf Zulaikhā, by Jāmī.

Ff. 150. Good nasta'līq. 1 Dhu 'l-Qa'da 976/17 April 1569. Printed many times. Ivanow 612 (21).

431 (p) **Or. 1683 (9)**

Fawā'id al-fu'ād, by Najm al-Dīn Ḥasan b. 'Alā' al-Dīn Sanjarī (d. *ca.* 727/1327).

Ff. 197. Clear nasta'līq. 21 Rajab 1215/8 Dec. 1800. Ivanow 239.

432 (p) **Or. 1684 (9)**

1. *Ṭūr-i ma'rifat*, by Mīrzā 'Abd al-Qādir Bīdil, (d. 1133/1720). Ethé I.O. 1686.

2. *Muḥīṭ-i a'ẓam*, by the same author. Ethé, I.O. 1682.

3. *Dīwān*, by Nāṣir 'Alī Sirhindī (d. 1108/1697). Ethé, I.O. 1639.

Ff. 204. 26 Rabī' 1 1146/6 Sept. 1733.

433 (p) **Or. 1685 (9)**

Dīwān, by Abū Isḥāq Muḥammad (Ibrāhīm) Bukhārī Shaukat (d. 1107/1695).

Ff. 202. Clear nasta'līq. 21 Rabī' I 1314/30 Aug. 1896. Ivanow 809.

434 (p) **Or. 1686 (9)**

A work on geography, incomplete at the beginning.

Ff. 86. Clear nasta'līq. Dhu 'l-Qa'da 1066/Aug.–Sept. 1656.

435 (p) **Or. 1687 (10)**

Dīwān, by Auḥad al-Dīn 'Alī Anwarī (fl. *ca.* 550/1155).

Ff. 208. Clear nasta'līq. 10/16th century. Lithographed several times. Ivanow 450.

436 (p) **Or. 1688 (11)**

Nuzhat al-qulūb, by Ḥamd Allāh b. Abī Bakr Mustaufī Qazwīnī (d. *ca.* 750/1349).

Ff. 204. Clear nasta'līq. Muḥarram 1103/Sept.–Oct. 1691. Miniatures. Lithographed at Bombay, 1894, printed (ed. G. Le Strange), London, 1915. Ivanow-Curzon 89.

437 (p) **Or. 1689 (12)**

Dīwān, by Barakāt.

Ff. 281. Clear nasta'līq. 1 Jumādā II 1231/29 April 1816.

438 (p) **Or. 1690 (14)**

Tadhkira-yi Muḥammad-Shāhī, by Bahman Qājār.

Ff. 213. Excellent nasta'līq. 13/19th century. Illuminated 'unwān, margins ruled throughout in gold and colours.

439 (p) **Or. 1691 (14)**

Tārīkh-i 'ālam-ārāy-i 'Abbāsī, by Iskandar Munshī (d. 1038/1628).

Ff. 346. Excellent nasta'līq. 10 Jumādā II 1071/10 Feb. 1661. Margins ruled throughout in gold and colours. Printed at Teheran, 1313–14/1896–7. Storey, p. 310, no. 387.

440 (p) **Or. 1694 (9)**

Tuḥfat al-'Irāqain, by Khāqānī. *See* no. 168 (1).

Ff. 120. Calligraphic nasta'līq. Ramaḍān 1305/May 1888. Fine gold illuminated 'unwān; margins ruled in gold and black; six miniatures.

441 (p) **Or. 1696 (7)**

Dīwān, by Fāryābī (d. 598/1201). *See* no. 167.

Ff. 150. Excellent calligraphic nasta'līq. 902/1496–7. Illuminated 'unwān and vignettes, margins ruled in gold and colours throughout.

442 (a) **Or. 1697 (10)**

Sharḥ al-Mukhtaṣar, by Faṣīḥ b. 'Abd al-Karīm al-Niẓāmī (fl. *ca.* 850/1446).

Ff. 72. Excellent calligraphic nasta'līq. 9/15th century. Excellent illuminated 'unwān; margins ruled throughout in gold and colours.

443 (p) **Or. 1698 (10)**

1. *Ilāhī-nāma*, ff. 7–86.
2. *Ushtur-nāma*, ff. 87–178.
3. *Bulbul-nāma*, ff. 179–94.
4. *Waṣlat-nāma*, ff. 195–212.
5. *Manṭiq al-ṭair*, ff. 213–66.
6. *Muṣībat-nāma*, ff. 267–346.
7. *Asrār-nāma*, ff. 347–382.

All by Farīd al-Dīn 'Aṭṭār.

Ff. 382. Clear ta'līq. 829/1425–6. Lithographed at Lucknow, 1872. Ivanow 477.

444 (a) **Or. 1701 (9)**

Al-Ṭibb al-Manṣūrī, by Abū Bakr al-Rāzī (d. 313/925). *See* no. 301.

Ff. 275. Clear naskh. 12/18th century.

445 (a) **Or. 1703 (10)**

Tuḥfat al-arīb wa-nuzhat al-labīb, by Abū Madyan Muḥammad b. Aḥmad al-Fāsī (d. 1181/1767).

Ff. 189. Excellent calligraphic maghribī. 9 Jumādā II 1265/2 May 1849. Brockelmann, Suppl. II, 690.

446 (a) **Or. 1704** (13)

Muqaddama nāfi'a fi 'l-'aqā'id, by Abu'l-Mawāhib 'Abd al-Wahhāb b. Aḥmad b. 'Alī al-Sha'rānī (d. 975/1565).

Ff. 8. Holograph. 3 Sha'bān 956/27 Aug. 1549.

447 (a) **Or. 1705** (8)

1. *Risāla fi 'l-samā' wa'l-raqṣ*, by Abu 'l-'Abbās Aḥmad b. Yūsuf al-Nā'ilī al-Fāsī al-Fihrī (d. 1021/1612). Ff. 1–7. No other copy appears to be recorded.

2. *Iqāmat al-ḥujja fi 'l-radd 'alā mā aḥdathahu 'l-mubtadi'a*, by Abū Muḥammad Aḥmad b. 'Abd al-Raḥmān al-Fishtālī (fl. 12/18th century). Ff. 8–13. Brockelmann, Suppl. II 696.

3. *Al-Munjalī fī taṭauwur al-walī*, by Jalāl al-Dīn al-Suyūṭī. Ff. 14–17*a*. Brockelmann II, 156; Suppl. II, 195.

4. *Juz'*, by Abu'l-'Abbās Aḥmad b. Aḥmad Ibn Aḥmad Bābā al-Ṣanhājī al-Sūdānī (d. 1036/1627). Ff. 17*b*–32. Brockelmann, Suppl. II, 716.

5. *Risāla fi 'l-dhikr*, by Aḥmad b. Yūsuf al-Fāsī. Ff. 33–37. No other copy appears to be recorded.

Ff. 37. Clear maghribī. 13/19th century.

448 (a) **Or. 1706** (9)

Al-Rasā'il al-ṣughrā, by Abū 'Abd Allāh Muḥammad b. Ibrāhīm Ibn 'Abbād al-Nafzī (d. 792/1390).

Ff. 53. Clear maghribī. 11/17th century. Brockelmann, Suppl. II, 358.

449 (a) **Or. 1707** (7)

Dalā'il al-khairāt, by al-Jazūlī (d. 870/1465). *See* no. 335 (1).

Ff. 116. Good naskh. 13/19th century. Some illumination.

450 (a) **Or. 1708** (9)

Al-Shuqrūnīya fi 'l-ṭibb, by Abū Muḥammad 'Abd al-Qādir Ibn Shuqrūn al-Miknāsī (fl. 11/17th century).

Ff. 24. Good maghribī. Shauwāl 1301/July–Aug. 1884. Margins ruled in red throughout. Brockelmann, Suppl. II, 714.

INDEX

References are to article not to page. Titles in italics. Name of persons include (among others) authors, former owners, and donors. Hyphen prefixed to a word indicates omission of definite article *ab*. Prefixes such as *Abū*, *Ibn*, *de*, *le*, *von* are disregarded in alphabetical arrangement.